OUR
BLESSED
BOOK

EVANGELIST
CALEB GARRAWAY

Our Blessed Book

Copyright © 2010 Caleb & Katie Garraway

ISBN: 978-0-9829105-6-6

Faithful Life Publishers
3335 Galaxy Way
North Fort Myers, FL 33903
www.FaithfulLifePublishers.com
info@FLPublishers.com

EVANGELISM MINISTRIES
Caleb & Katie Garraway
5517 NW 23rd Street
Oklahoma City, OK 73127

www.thegarrawayfamily.com

Scripture quotations are from the Authorized King James Version

Printed in the United States of America

18 17 16 15 14 13 12 11 10   1 2 3 4 5

For the prophecy came not in old time by the will of man:
but holy men of God spake as they were moved
by the Holy Ghost.
2 Peter 1:21

Being born again, not of corruptible seed,
but of incorruptible, by the word of God,
which liveth and abideth for ever.
For all flesh is as grass, and all the glory of man
as the flower of grass. The grass withereth,
and the flower hereof falleth away:
But the word of the Lord endureth for ever.
And this is the word which by the gospel
is preached unto you.
1 Peter 1:23-25

Behold, I have longed after thy precepts:
quicken me in thy righteousness.
Psalm 119:40

TABLE OF CONTENTS

INTRODUCTION

The Bible is the Word of God. Each and every one of us,saved or unsaved, need the words of God He has painstakingly written and preserved for us in order to behold His truth. The Devil has for many centuries now tried his best to "stamp out" the Word of God but has been unsuccessful. He does what he can to rip it apart, doctrine by doctrine. He has inflated the market with all sorts of false translations of the Bible to get people onto the wrong track and to read the wrong Bible, because he knows that the Bible holds *the answer.*

God wrote the Bible for the human race for two reasons. First of all, God's Word teaches us how we can know for sure that when we die that Heaven will be our home. God reveals how salvation has been made possible for us through the death, burial, and resurrection of Christ. We would be quite *eternally hopeless* without the Bible. And, secondly, the Bible shows us how to effectively live: how to have a good life, how to avoid the snares of Satan and sin, how to please our Heavenly Father, and how to walk in His blessings.

In order to effectively live our life according to how God wants us to live it and to know what the will of God is for our lives, we *must* have the Word of God as our foundational basis. For without the Bible, what would we do? Where would we be today? How could we live our lives? How could we do what is right and pleasing to our Heavenly Father? Without the Bible there would be no guidelines as we walk the Christian life.

The Devil also understands that God speaks to us through reading His Word. God will use verses or passages of Scripture to encourage us, strengthen us, challenge us, stir us, convict us, or change us. He does not appear to Christians in dreams or visions any more, because we have a completed Word of God.

How exciting it is to realize that God—the One Who created this universe—wants to spend time with *you*, speaking to you through the Bible (or messages from the Bible) and listening to you talk to Him in prayer. He wants to have constant fellowship and communication with you!

The Devil recognizes that the Word of God is the basis for our beliefs. Everything that we as Christians and Fundamental Baptists believe is totally based on the doctrines, teachings, and principles of God's Word. If there were no Bible, there would be nothing to believe in. If there were no Bible, there would be no "absolutes."

The Devil is trying to shake Christianity at its core by destroying its Foundation—the Word of God. He also is trying to convince the average Christian, a majority of the next generation Christians, and society in general that the Bible has NOT been inspired or preserved by God. Therefore, before we can understand the teachings of the Word of God, we really need to *first* believe that the Bible (specifically the *King James Bible* for the English-speaking people) is truly the inspired, preserved Word of God. What good is it to learn what the Bible teaches when you don't even know that the Bible truly *is* God's precious words?

I know what is going through your mind, Christian and fellow young person, because I have been where you're at. I know you are wondering whether or not the Bible *truly is* God's inspired, preserved Word; and I know you are wondering whether the King James Bible is actually God's Word for the English-speaking people. No, I didn't say that you are *doubting* that it is, but down deep in your heart you might be *wondering* how or why it is. All the questions you might have will be answered, and your genuine curiosity will be satisfied if you continue to read this book. We want to break it down to simply understand why God's Word is truly God's Word!

We will be following the Word of God's thin white line of a trail throughout history:

- *Beginning with God originally speaking the Bible's very words to His writers into human existence,*

- *continuing in seeing how Satan has provided four counterfeit inspiration theories,*

- *stopping to look at various proofs permanently engrained into all creation of how the Bible must have been inspired by God,*

- *moving onward to see how God phenomenally and miraculously preserved His Word,*

- *discovering the historical and doctrinal errors of the Apocrypha, the "missing" books of the Bible,*

- *examining the origins of the King James Bible—the only inspired, preserved Word of God for English speaking people,*

- *seeing issues with the New King James Version,*

- *noting the perversions of all of the other English versions introduced by Satan, and*

- *reading what other great figures in history have said about the Word of God and its importance.*

It is very important to understand these things and have them solidified in our minds and our hearts. Before we can truly "maintain the cause" for Christ, before we can *"continue…in the things which thou hast learned and hast been assured of,"* as Paul challenged Timothy (II Timothy 3:14), and before we can know what we believe and why we believe it, we must first have the confidence that God's Word truly is God's words.

Our Blessed Book is not a book of criticism but a book of truth. The Bible is something we must protect and defend. Therefore, in order to know right from wrong, we must examine how the right is different from the wrong. We must understand why the wrong will never be right, and why it should *never* be allowed or accepted. This book is not intended to be derogatory but to be helpful—encouraging believers to know the infallibility of their Bible and to know that the King James Bible is the inspired, preserved Word of God for the English speaking people.

By the end of this book, I know that you will clearly see that the Bible (specifically the King James Bible for the English-speaking people) is most definitely the Word of God.

God bless you!

[signature]

I Cor 16:13

CHAPTER I

THE INSPIRATION OF THE BIBLE

"In the beginning God…" (Genesis 1:1) God is the beginning of all things. He is the beginning of **creation**. Over 6,000 years ago, He created the vast universe, speaking and flinging the heavens into existence. In the midst of all this matchless glory and space, He formed a single, small speck of a planet that He called Earth, created all life upon it, even forming his highest creation after His own image, calling him Man. This world would be *the primary focus* of the Almighty Jehovah. Soon His creation fell in the Garden of Eden and sinned, breaking the commandment of God. Man began to utterly reject their Maker's authority and plunged themselves into sin and death to dwell in darkness…forever. The penalty of sin was death—a death separated from God in Hell for all of eternity. But this was not God's desire.

Therefore, God is the beginning of **salvation**. With incomprehensible love, God promised humanity in the first few chapters of the Bible that He would one day send a Sacrifice—the Messiah—to give His life and pay for the sins of the world. Only One could do this: God's only begotten sinless Son. Since the beginning of time, the Son of God was eager to give Himself for the precious lives of the world. I Peter 1:18-20 teaches us, *"Forasmuch as ye know that ye were not redeemed with corruptible* *things, as silver and gold, from your vain conversation received by tradition from your fathers; But with the precious blood of Christ, as of a lamb without blemish and without spot: Who verily was foreordained before the foundation of the world, but was manifest in these last times for you."* So God sent Christ willingly to such a *trite obscure place* to die, shed His blood, and rise again on the third day to give us the opportunity to go to Heaven.

Humanity needed to hear of this "plan of redemption" and this "gift of eternal life" that God had made available for them. They needed to hear that there was *hope.* God decided to write a "letter" to show them the way and to give an open invitation for all to come Him and partake of salvation. Therefore in the beginning, He wrote *the Bible.* John 1:1-2 relates to us: *"In the beginning was the Word, and the Word was with God, and the Word was God. The same was in the beginning with God."* God was the beginning of **inspiration**. He wrote every word and every part of the Bible in the beginning of time, then gave it to man throughout early history until it was complete around A.D. 100.

The word *inspiration* means "God-breathed." II Timothy 3:16 tells us that "**All** scripture is given by inspiration of God." In other words, "All scripture is God-breathed," or more effectively stated: "All scripture is given by the *breath* of God." God in His sovereignty has breathed out *every single word that He wanted written down.* Throughout 1500 years, He spoke through forty specially chosen and prepared men of God. God used these men as instruments, and He breathed *through* them His words that He wanted penned for mankind.

Although these men were used by God for one specific purpose, each of them, were distinctly different. This is a blessing to me, because that means that God can use anybody! They all were different in the way they looked. Some were probably short; some were tall; some were rotund; and, I am sure, some were skinny. Some had flat noses while others had beaky noses. Each had a different shaped head with various hairlines. These men had physical differences.

Each of them had a different relationship with their Heavenly Father. David was a man after God's own heart, while

Nebuchadnezzar might have been worldly, surrounded by a lavish empire. Peter cursed his Lord but got right with God through weeping and rededication, then experienced a Holy Ghost sent revival called Pentecost. Some were prophets receiving various revelations from the Lord; while others were like Jonah, who ran from the calling of God and was bitter that wicked heathen repented from their sins.

All of them had different occupations. Amos and Micah were farmers. Hosea was a herdsman. Luke was a doctor. Paul was an evangelist, a tentmaker, and a former murderer. David, Solomon, and Nebuchadnezzar were kings of nations and empires. Peter, James, and John were fisherman. Moses was the adopted grandson of Pharaoh and was a shepherd of sheep for forty years in the desert of the Sinai Peninsula. Daniel was a prime minister. Matthew was a tax collector, a publican. Nehemiah was a cupbearer for King Artexerxes, emperor of the Medes' and Persian Empire compassing most of the known world at that time. Ezra was a priest.

Each of these men talked differently. Peter, James, and John spoke with the drawl of a Nazarene fisherman (though not after the style of a fisherman). Nebuchadnezzar spoke with masterful eloquence of an emperor in Chaldean. Daniel spoke Chaldean, Hebrew, and possibly other languages with polished refinement as the king's direct ambassador. Hosea talked like a herdsman—a cattle rancher.

Each of these men walked differently. David carried himself with the grace of a king. Peter strolled like a fisherman. Hosea walked as a rough herdsman. You can use your imagination as see how all were not the same.

Each of these men smelled differently. Peter, James, and John—embellished with the fragrance of reeking fish—did not smell the same as the kings who wrote passages of the Bible! Moses with the smell of the desert did not resemble the smell of Luke with his salve and doctor supplies.

I am sure they all thought differently.

They all probably did not like the same foods.

They were from different families and different Jewish

tribes. Some were Gentiles.

These men were **different** from each other, yet God used these forty different individuals to pen the words that He wanted written down so that you and I might read them today in the Scriptures.

Isn't it amazing that though these men were *different*, all the books of the Bible correlate with each other? Isn't it amazing that each of these men lived in *different* time periods, some hundreds of years apart; yet each of these books fit together like pieces of a puzzle? All these men were *different*, but they had one thing in common. They were **all** inspired by **the same LORD God** to write down His words that He wanted penned.

These men were human beings just like us. These men were men specially used of God to pen the Holy Scriptures. As we read the Scriptures, we can see that each book of the Bible penned by a different author is of a different flavor. Each book of the Bible is not of the same style. They are of *different* styles and of *different* tastes. This is because God used the personalities of these men when He spoke to them to write down His words. God did not use them as robots! He did not mechanically dictate what He wanted them to write down, but He spoke *through* them (through their style and taste) as these men were moved by the Holy Spirit of God. II Peter 1:21 tells us: *"For the prophecy came not in old time by the will of man: **but** holy men of God spake as they were moved by the Holy Ghost."* Notice God spoke *through* them and not *to* them.

To understand this more easily, let's use an example. Let's say that I had four different musical instruments in front of me such as a flute, a bagpipe, a trumpet, and a harmonica. *Certainly* each of these instruments look different, each of them play differently, and each of them make a different sound. **Nevertheless,** if I played on each of them individually, *who is playing these instruments?* Obviously, I am. As I play each instrument, I am breathing *through* them to play the tune I want played. Suppose that I am playing the hymn "Amazing Grace." As I play each of these different instruments, it makes a different musical *sound*. However, they are all producing the *same* tune of "Amazing Grace." Yet a flute does not sound like a trumpet, and a bagpipe does not sound like a harmonica! A trumpet does not sound like a harmonica, and a flute does not sound like a bagpipe! *None of these instruments sound the same!* Each of them are *different.* However, they are producing the same tune, and I am the one still breathing through them to play them.

This same illustration can be applied to God and His men He used to write the Bible. He inspired these men…God breathed *through* these men (as I breathed through those instruments) to pen His Word. Meanwhile, God was "playing" one "song" through them. The one central theme of the Bible is *Jesus Christ.* This "song" shows how Christ *first* came as the Lamb of God to become a Sacrifice and the Saviour, but how He is coming a *second* time as the Lion of Judah, the Sovereign!

The whole Bible deals with how man is lost and is in need of the Saviour, Jesus Christ. The Old Testament shows God's plan for man's salvation through Jesus. All the sacrifices described in Exodus, Leviticus, and Numbers point toward the sacrifice Christ would one day make once and for all. The prophecies in the prophetic books speak of His birth, His life, His death, and His Second Coming. The Gospels of the New Testament give us a detailed account of His earthly ministry, His death, His burial, and His resurrection. The Epistles deal with *living and preaching* for Christ. Revelation deals with the judgment Jesus will pour out upon a wicked world, His second coming to this earth, His millennial reign, and the final days before eternity.

God has given us His Word, writing it for us through forty different men. He *inspired* them, *breathing **through** them* the words that He wanted written. God breathed out ***the very words*** of the Bible to His men to write down. This is what we believe. We call it the verbal plenary inspiration of Scripture. This is an important doctrine for Fundamentalists and Bible believers.

In *"verbal plenary inspiration,"* the word *verbal* means "word for word"—the Bible was delivered *word for word* from God's mouth. Charles Spurgeon, the Prince of Preachers, said it this way once: *"This [Bible] is the writing of the living God: each letter was penned with an Almighty finger; each word in it dropped from the everlasting lips; each sentence was dictated by the Holy Spirit."*

The word *scripture* used in the Bible means "the *actual writings.*" The Bible says in II Timothy 3:16, as we have already seen, "All *scripture* [the actual writings] is given by inspiration of God." Acts 1:16 says, "This *scripture* [the actual writings] which *the Holy Ghost* **by the mouth of David** *spake."*

There are liberal Bible scholars who take Acts 1:16 very literally in the sense that the Holy Spirit said what *He* wanted to say by David's mouth. They call it *mechanical dictation. Mechanical dictation* means that the Bible writers were only dictaphones or typewriters; hence, their cultural and personality factors did not enter into their works. Of course, this is not true, because we've already seen that Paul's writings were different in style from those of John, Peter, Daniel, Moses, or David. Yes, God did give these men the words to say, but, at the *same* time, God spoke *through* them. When God spoke, His men *did not* suddenly change personalities and become the voice of the Holy Spirit. God used these men just like they were, breathing His words *through* them.

For instance, a secretary never becomes a robot when she writes down what her boss or her authority is directing for her to write. She still remains a *human being* with all of her mind and all of her personality. The *same* is true with God and His men that were chosen to write down His words. These men did *not* just become robots or mechanical writers. Louis Gaussen who wrote *The Divine Inspiration of Scriptures* in the 1800's said, *"Their intellectual faculties were at the time directed, not suspended. They knew, they felt, they willed, they recollected, they understood, they approved."*

In *"verbal plenary inspiration"*, the word *plenary* means "full." We believe that the "full" Bible was written by God. God breathed out *every word and every part* of Scripture that He had His men write down. Again, we can look at II Timothy 3:16: "***All scripture* is given by *inspiration* of God." In other words, "*Every word* of** Scripture *is given* **by the breath of God.***"* Proverbs 30:5 tells us, "***Every word*** of God is pure ("clean or undefiled")." Matthew 4:4 says, "It is written, Man shall not live by bread alone, but by **every word** that *proceedeth out of the mouth of God."* Every word and every part of the Bible has been God-breathed.

What a blessing to realize that God has taken the time to give us *a Book that He wrote!* We ought to thank Him for that! This should excite us to praise His name with spiritual enthusiasm!

Take a look at what a few men of God have said about *verbal plenary inspiration.*

"That this inspiration should extend to the **very words** seems most natural since the purpose of inspiration is to secure an infallible record of truth. Thoughts and words are so inseparably connected that as a rule a change in words means a change in thought."
—*Loraine Boettner*

"It has always been a matter of profound surprise to me that anybody should ever question the **verbal inspiration** of the Bible."
—*B. H. Carroll*

"Scripture wants us to receive **all its words** as **words chosen by God** and therefore expressing the thought so perfectly and infallibly as only God can express it."
—*Theodore Engelder*

"Let it be observed, that not the matter of the Scriptures only, but the **very words** in which they are writing are of God."
—*John Gill*

"It is safe to say that there is no doctrine… which has been so widely held through the ages of Church history as that of **verbal inspiration**."
—*R. Laird Harris*

"I know the Bible is **inspired** *because it **inspires** me.*"
—*D. L. Moody*

"If the **words** were not wholly God's, then their teaching would not be wholly God's."

—*J. I. Packer*

"If the **words** godhead, election, redemption, imputation, regeneration, propitiation, sacrifice, atonement, faith, repentance, justification, sanctification, adoption, resurrection, heaven, Hell, etc., were not inspired and infallible, then everything essential to Christian faith and life may be only *old wives' fables*. Without certainty and divine authority in the **words** of Scripture, it is patently impossible to believe in the things, or even to know the will of God, for our salvation."

—*MacIntosh*

"Inspiration does not consist in mere divine guidance and protection against error, but is a divine supplying or divine giving of the **very words** that constitute Scripture."

—*Francis Pieper*

"Verbal inspiration is at the heart of what inspiration means. The **words** which are written in Scripture are the **words of God** himself."

—*Clark H. Pinnock*

"Just as far as the thoughts of Scripture relating to any element or topic whatsoever are inspired, the **words** in which those thoughts are expressed must be inspired also. Every element of Scripture, whether doctrine or history, of which God has guaranteed the infallibility, must be infallible in its **verbal** expression."

—*Benjamin B. Warfield*

"The Bible must be the invention either of good men or

angels, bad men or devils, or of God.

> 1. It could not be the invention of good men or angels; for they neither would nor could make a book, and tell lies all the time they were writing it, saying, 'Thus saith the Lord,' when it was their own invention.
>
> 2. It could not be the invention of bad men or devils; for they would not make a book which commands all duty, forbids all sin, and condemns their souls to Hell to all eternity.
>
> 3. Therefore, I draw the conclusion, that *the Bible must be given by **divine inspiration**.*"
>
> —*John Wesley*

What we just discussed was *what Biblical inspiration is.* Biblical inspiration is of the LORD God Almighty. Biblical inspiration is verbal plenary inspiration. Now let's look at *what Biblical inspiration is **not**.*

There are several different meanings for inspiration other than the term used for Biblical inspiration. For example, I think of the athlete who is *inspired* to run the Boston marathon because his passionate desire is to win that race. I think of wonderful musical pieces by Mozart, Beethoven, Bach, Hayden, and Vivaldi. These men have written marvelous classical pieces of complex music, but they were not God breathed. I think of the great works of literature written by famous authors throughout the centuries. Yes, these masterpieces are great books, but God did not breath them out as He did the Bible. For instance, I was *inspired* to write this book that you are now reading, but this book is *not **God breathed!** No other book **except the Sacred Holy Scriptures** has been written in the same fashion.*

Whenever or wherever there is God's truth, the Devil *always* tries to counterattack it with one or more lies. We can see for example: Christmas and Easter. Most people [especially the younger generation] have no idea what Christmas is *really all about.* They think it is a time of exchanging gifts, Santa Claus, food, fun, and partying. The same thing has happened with Easter. People are sidetracked from the real thing with the Easter Bunny, egg hunts, and picnics.

As much as Satan has tried to counterattack these two very important Christian days, he has tried to counterattack the Bible through two means: by flooding the markets with false versions of the Bible and by introducing four false beliefs of how the Bible was inspired. These four beliefs are natural inspiration, partial inspiration, conceptual inspiration, and the "encounter theory" inspiration.

Natural Inspiration

This counterfeit theological philosophy teaches that the Bible is only as inspired as man's highest classical works of literature were. For instance, the Bible then would only be as inspired as any of Shakespeare's works or as the Handel's *Messiah*. Of course, this is not true. Yes, the works of Shakespeare were inspired but *not* inspired by God. Yes, Handel's *Messiah* is a fantastic work, and he must have been truly "inspired" to write such an intricate composition, since he wrote it in less than a month's time! ...But it was not *God breathed.* Natural inspiration says that the Bible is only as inspired as the works of man are, but we understand that God never breathed the words of those great literature masterpieces or breathed the musical tunes of those great musical compositions.

Natural inspiration is nothing more than *human* inspiration. The modernists, the atheists, the liberals, and all the rest of the anti-God crowd are trying their best to get *others* to believe in natural inspiration to successfully blind-fold them into believing that the Bible is only *humanly* inspired and is just another "book" and not really from God.

This false theory of inspiration "slaps God in the face, "because when you deny His Word, making it just like another book, you deny **Him!** The atheists, the liberals, and anti-Bible religions of today gladly welcome this type of inspiration to get rid of (in their minds) and to easily excuse away the Bible. If they can excuse away the Bible, they can excuse away God. If they can excuse away the Bible, they can excuse away Hell and all type of wickedness. They can formulate their own doctrines and their own beliefs and can believe whatever they want to believe in, *because the Bible is only humanly or naturally inspired.*

Have you ever met people like that before? If you were to ask them what they believe about the Bible, I am almost positive they would respond that it's either a fairy tale with good stories and morals, or a book with lessons that men have contributed to for thousands of years. In some way they will deny that God wrote it and say it is not divinely inspired. If they can deny the Bible in their minds, then they can easily deny that there is a God.

PARTIAL INSPIRATION

This second false theological belief about inspiration teaches that the Bible is only **partially** inspired in certain portions and not **totally** inspired word-for-word. No, the people who believe this do not go all the way to the left and say that the Bible is not inspired at all or is just "naturally inspired" like any other book that man has written. They do realize that there was some element of God involved. However, they still do not believe that the Bible is totally and truly God's inspired Word. Various religions and denominations believe this in order to make the Bible fit their system of beliefs.

The "partial inspiration" theory teaches that the Bible only *contains* the Word of God and is only *partially* inspired; therefore, some of the Bible is truth, and some of it is error. This leads us to the question: "So what then *is* truth, and what *is* error?" Basically, it's now man's decision, and it's left up to man's discretion. Truth is whatever **man** *decides* to be truth. Error is whatever **man** *decides* to be error. Man decides what *is* inspired and what is *not* inspired. This makes man higher than God. This is the philosophy of humanism—that man is God—in action.

First of all, we can refute this false form of inspiration with the simple fact that the Bible claims to be **totally** inspired by God. II Timothy 3:16 tells us, "**All scripture** [every word and every part] is given by inspiration of God." Friend, the Bible does not just *contain* the Word of God, but it *is* the Word of God—every word and every part: **all scripture!**

Secondly, we can logically reason that if the Holy Spirit had inspired *some* of the Bible, why could He not have inspired *all* of it? For example, if we can trust God's Word for our salvation, *then why can't we trust God's Word about how we are supposed to live our lives?* If we can trust in the Bible for our daily strength, then why can't we trust in the Bible for our daily correction? But no, since some people don't like specific passages of Scripture that "step on our toes" or convict them, they say that those portions are not inspired by God and excuse them away.

You see, through this wrong concept of inspiration, man can choose what is right and what is wrong, so on and so forth. But when did we become God to say what is truth and what is not truth? Romans 11:33-36, "O the depth of the riches both of the wisdom and knowledge of God! how unsearchable are his judgments, and his ways past finding out! **For who hath known the mind of the Lord? or who hath been his counsellor?** *Or who hath first given to him,* and it shall be recompensed unto him again? For of him, and through him, and to him, are all things:" This means that the only reason why we are alive and well on this planet today is because of God. *And how **dare** we defy His name and say what is inspired and what is not!*

This is just another theory that Satan is using to trip up weak Christians in the faith or to keep those who believe this type of inspiration blinded from the real truth.

CONCEPTUAL INSPIRATION

Conceptual inspiration teaches that God only inspired the *thoughts* that He gave the men to write the Bible, and then *those men* in their *own words* wrote down those thoughts that God had given him. As we know, the Bible teaches the **verbal plenary inspiration** of Scripture, meaning that every word and every part of the Bible has been God-breathed. Notice He inspired *every* **word** and *every* **part**. *Not just the concepts. Not just the thoughts. But the **words**!*

What is interesting is that in some instances in the Bible the writers *did **not** understand what they were writing!* Therefore, if God only gave these men the thoughts or just the concepts how could they write the words? For example, Daniel says in Daniel 7:15-16 when he was receiving from God the visions of future times, *"I Daniel was grieved in my spirit in the midst of my body, and the visions of my head troubled me. I came near unto one of them that stood by, and asked him the truth of all this. So he told me, and made me know the interpretation of the things."* In another instance in Daniel 8:27, Daniel said, *"I was astonished at the vision, but none understood it."* Lastly, Daniel says again in Daniel 12:8-9, *"And I heard, **but I understood not**: then said I, O my Lord, what shall be the end of these things? And he said, Go thy way, Daniel: for the words are closed up and sealed till the time of the end."* Peter also tells us in his first epistle in chapter 1 verses 10 and 12, *"Of which salvation the prophets have enquired and searched diligently.... Unto whom it was revealed, that not unto themselves, but unto us they did minister."*

It is evident that God inspired the words and not just the thoughts that He gave His men, for if God only inspired the thoughts, *then how could they understand what to write down on paper?*

Think of it this way. Let's say you walked into physics class on the first day and your teacher gave you and your friends an overview of that subject and your homework assignment for the next week was to write a detailed book on it. How could you possibly write a detailed book on physics, when you don't even understand it, and you haven't even taken that class yet? *The same is true with the Bible.* That is why we believe God inspired **the words** and not merely the concepts or the thoughts that He gave His men.

Encounter Theory Inspiration

The last false theory of inspiration says that the Bible *becomes* the Word of God as you read it. It is, in a sense, just a "book." It is not necessarily the Word of God, **but** it *will* become the Word of God **only** when it personally speaks to you.

Well, *that* is nonsense! For instance, let's say that a certain verse speaks to my heart and it doesn't speak to *your* heart. Is it still inspired then? On the other hand, some verse of Scripture may put you highly under conviction, and I may just read over the verse without thinking about it. *Is that verse in the Bible therefore inspired, or not?* Of course it is. Just because the long lists of names in the Book of Numbers does not speak to our hearts or put us under conviction *does not mean* that it is not inspired of God. It is most certainly inspired, because God took the time and put it in His Word. God's Word *is* truth as the Bible says in John 17:17, "Thy *word* is truth."

It is pretty crazy what the Devil tries to put out there for people. What is sad is that people fall for it and believe it with all of their hearts.

Conclusion

We can refute all those counterfeit theories with **one** simple verse of Scripture. This verse is II Timothy 3:16: *"All scripture is given by inspiration of God."* **I encourage you to memorize it.**

Man may say that inspiration is natural. But God says, "All scripture is **given by inspiration of *God*.**"

Man may say, "Only **parts** of the Bible are inspired." But God said, "**All** scripture [**every** *word* and **every** *part*] is given by inspiration of God."

Man may say, "Well, only the **thoughts** were inspired by God to the human writers." But God says, "All **scripture** [the **writings**—the **actual words** that were penned] is given by inspiration of God."

Man may say, "The Bible only **becomes** the Word of God when it speaks to you when you read it." But God has given in His word that, "**All** scripture is given by inspiration of God, and is **profitable**."

Charles Haddon Spurgeon, the great "Prince of Preachers," said it this way concerning verbal plenary inspiration: "Never let us forget this. The **whole** of the Bible is *inspired,* and is to be devoutly received as the *infallible* truth of God. Get away from this, and *we have nothing left to hold by.* Whatever we do, let us never give up the Bible. *Those who would weaken our reverence for it are **our worst enemies**.*" Those that mock God's Word and try to downgrade God given inspiration are our worst enemies. That means the modernist is your enemy, the atheist is your enemy, the liberal is your enemy, the Satanist is your enemy, the agnostic is your enemy, and various other "religionists" are your enemies! Watch out for them! They are going to try their best to discourage you, ridicule you, and tear you down.

This is why it's important that you know what you believe and why you believe it as a Christian…so that you might be able to effectively filter out what others (who are anti-God and twist His truths) have to say about their false views of the Bible! Listen, if you know what the Bible says, *then you'll not have to* **worry** *about the things men come up with,* because you already **know** the truth, and that it is *impossible* for God to lie.

Friend, "Let **God** be true, and *every man a* **liar.**" (Romans 3:4)

CHAPTER II

PROOFS OF BIBLICAL INSPIRATION

"No book in the world has been so misjudged as the Bible. Men judge it without reading it. Or perhaps they read a bit here and a bit there, and then close it, saying: "It is so dark and mysterious!" You take a book now-a-days and read it: "Well," you say, "I have only read it through once, not very carefully, and I should not like to give an opinion;" yet people take up God's book, read a few pages, and condemn the whole of it. Of all the skeptics and infidels I have ever met speaking against the Bible, I have never met one who read it through. There may be such men, but I have never met them. It is simply an excuse. There is no man living who will stand up before God and say that the Bible kept him out of the kingdom." – D. L. Moody

Most of the liberals, atheists, and skeptics in society today like to make fun of the Word of God, especially the God-given inspiration of the Scriptures. Therefore, as Bible-believing Christians, it is important for us to know proofs of why the Bible truly is and has to be inspired by God—proofs that would show that the Bible is far above any human work and greater than any accomplishment of human imagination. There are too many infallible truths that prove the Bible as *God's Word*.

You know, there are *many* people in this world that are truly searching for the truth. Yes, sometimes they will badmouth you and God's Word on the *outside* (especially when they are with their friends), **but** if you took the time and talked with them on a friendly, Christ-like, one-on-one basis, you'll find out that they are really searching for something. Take advantage of this and talk with them in compassion. Most of the time, people form their opinions about Christianity, church, salvation, and doctrines, because nobody has ever shown them that the Bible truly is *the inspired, preserved Word of God*. God will give you opportunities to talk to people like this. No, this is **not** an "argument" time but a "reasoning" time—a time for *you* to lovingly show them where they are wrong (not with an attitude of trying to prove your point). It is a time when you can neutrally show them from the Bible what the *Bible* says—not what religion or denominations say—and also relate to them what history, science, and other areas of proofs have to say about Biblical inspiration, as we will discuss in a moment.

When the skeptics of Biblical inspiration look at the "records," they have to realize—they *have* to realize—that God's Word truly *had* to be inspired by God. Yes, many have tried to downgrade the inspiration of the Bible, but God throughout the ages of time has always proved to those skeptics that criticize that His Word is true.

I believe that God has presented five simple proofs to show that the Bible is truly His inspired Word.

- *The Bible claims it*
- *History and Time reveal it*
- *Fulfilled Prophecies confirm it*
- *Science agrees with it*
- *Its changing of lives makes you believe it*

I hope that you will be able to grab hold of these proofs and someday use them to reach a skeptic or some other lost soul for Christ, explaining to them how the Bible is truly God's inspired Word. Remember, if a person does not believe that the Bible is the Word of God, they will not be able to truly believe salvation! We *must* know what we believe and why we believe it so that we can effectively witness to the skeptic and get them saved in the end.

THE BIBLE CLAIMS IT

It is as simple as that! The Bible *claims* to be inspired by God. Some may believe this proof is absurd because you supposedly "go around in circles with it." Such as, "The Bible is God's Word because it claims to be inspired, and the Bible claims to be inspired because it is *God's* Word (and God can't lie, etc.)." This might *appear* to be circular logic; but, if you have ever studied it out, the Bible is one of *few* books that has ever claimed to be written by God or a "god."

(Please don't misunderstand me. *Only the Word of God was written by God, and **nothing else**.* The other religious books—the Book of Mormon and the Qur'an—that claim to be written by [G]od, rather, a "*god*", are a product of Satan and are **NOT** written by Jehovah God, the Only Almighty Sovereign.)

History has shown that *other* so-called "God-inspired" books have either not stood the test of time *or* are somehow inferior to God's true holiness and perfection. God is not inferior; He is superior. He produces superior things without corruptions and inaccuracies. Those other books that claim to be inspired by God such as the Book of Mormon and the Qur'an are full of historical inaccuracies and twists of the truth.

The Book of Mormon is a work of plagiarism and man-made accounts. Many portions of its scripture are directly taken out of the King James Bible. Back in the 1820's when Joseph Smith "translated" the Book of Mormon from the "golden tablets" he found near Palmyra, New York, containing a new "Word of God," people in America spoke Elizabethan English. Smith desired to keep the Book of Mormon in the flare of the early 1600's King James

English used in the Bible. But his "English" style wasn't the greatest and the Book of Mormon wound up being full of grammatical inaccuracies, *except* those portions that were replications of the King James Bible.

In the Book of Mormon, Smith also got his dates mixed up. In Alma 46:15, believers are called "Christians" in about 73 BC, which contradicts both common sense and Acts 11:26 when they were *first* called "Christians" at Antioch *some time after Christ's ascension*. I Nephi 22:15 quotes from Malachi 4:1 even though Malachi wasn't written until about 160 years after the supposed events of I Nephi.

It's interesting how the Book of Mormon was translated. Joseph Smith put a magical "seer" stone into a hat, and then buried his face in the hat to exclude the light. Next, words in "reformed Egyptian" (no such language is known to exist) magically appeared with their translation, and Smith spoke the translation to a scribe who wrote it down. This is very different from how the King James Bible was translated into English. This will be discussed in further detail in a later chapter.

Interestingly, the book *History of Joseph Smith,* written by Joseph Smith's mother, Lucy Mack Smith, states on page 85: *"During our evening conversations, Joseph would occasionally give us some of the most amusing recitals that could be imagined. He would describe the ancient inhabitants of this continent, their dress, mode of traveling, and the animals upon which they rode; their cities, their buildings, with every particular; their mode of warfare; and also their religious worship. This he would do with as much ease, seemingly, as if he had spent his whole life among them."* So, how is it that Joseph Smith told these stories several years before he allegedly found the golden plates and wrote The Book of Mormon?

The Book of Mormon is advertised by the Church of Jesus Christ of Latter-Day Saints as "another testament of Jesus Christ" and specifically of the account of his supposed visit to the American continent, during His 40 days after His resurrection and before His ascension back to Heaven. There have been no traces of any of these things. Many scholars and people have searched known history of the Americas for evidence that the Book of Mormon is true, as has similarly been done with the Bible in the Middle East. The archeological evidence for the Bible is so overwhelming that even a former skeptic such as the great archeologist Sir William Ramsey became converted to Christian belief. But the archeological evidence against Mormon claims is so devastating that prominent Mormon archeologist Thomas Stewart Ferguson quit the Mormon Church and repudiated its prophet. While archeology findings continue to prove the Bible to be accurate, evidence for claims made in the Book of Mormon continue to be lacking.

The Smithsonian Institute issued a statement regarding the Book of Mormon. *"The Smithsonian Institution has never used the Book of Mormon in any way as a scientific guide. Smithsonian archaeologists see no direct connection between the archaeology of the New World and the subject matter of the book."*

According to the Smithsonian Institute in Washington, D.C., the following items (which, according to The Book of Mormon, existed in the Americas between 600 B.C. and 421 A.D.) have absolutely no evidence for existing in the Americas during that time:

- Silk—*Alma 4:6, Nephi 13:7, Alma 1:29*
- Horses—*Enos 1:21, Alma 18:9, III Nephi 3:1, Nephi 18:25*
- Steel—*Jarom 1:8, 2 Nephi 5:15,16, 1 Nephi 4:9, 16:18*
- Iron—*II Nephi 5:15, 20:34, Jarom 1:8, Mosiah 11:8*
- Coins—*Alma 11:5-19*
- Donkeys—*I Nephi 18:25, Mosiah 5:14, 12:5*
- Cattle, Cow, and Oxen—*Enos 1:21; III Nephi 3:22; Nephi 18:25*
- Pigs—*III Nephi 7:8*
- Grain and Wheat—*Mosiah 9:9; Helaman 11:17*

If The Book of Mormon is true, certainly some evidence for the items mentioned above should have been unearthed by modern-day archeologists. But should the objects of steel, iron, and brass that are mentioned throughout The Book of Mormon been found? NO. Has the Mormon church uncovered even one coin as mentioned in the book of Alma? NO. Mormon 6:9-15 states that many thousands of men fought a great battle armed with swords, bows, arrows and axes, but have archaeologists discovered any of these items dating back to that time period on this continent? NO. And there are a number of other discrepancies in the Book of Mormon. Why haven't we found any evidence?

Dr. Hugh Nibley of Brigham Young University (one of the greatest scholars in the church) declares: *"The Book of Mormon can and should be tested. It invites criticism."* Tenth president of the Mormon church, Joseph Fielding Smith things that the evidence for it *"internally and externally is overwhelming."* And the evidence is overwhelming…overwhelmingly showing us that the Book of Mormon **could not have been inspired by God**.

There are many issues with the Qur'an. The Qur'an is confused chronologically, saying that Ezekiel was in Judges, that Jonah and Samson were after Jesus Christ, and that Mary the mother of Jesus was the sister of Miriam, the sister of Moses and Aaron! The Qur'an says that Noah's **son** [notice it is singular] perished in the flood. The Qur'an teaches that Noah's ark rested on a Mt. Judi and not Mt. Ararat. The Qur'an teaches that Allah gave Abram the city of Mecca. The Qur'an says that John the Baptist's father, Zechariah, was only deaf and dumb *three* nights, and not the whole course of Elizabeth's pregnancy as the Holy Word of God teaches. These are just a few of the inaccuracies of the Qur'an.

The Qur'an teaches that there is only *one* god called Allah, and his name is **not** Jehovah God. The Muslims will try to convince you that "he" is the same being, but they are not. There is a great difference between Allah and Jehovah God. Twenty-four times the Qur'an repeats the concept of Surah 2:190, "For allah loveth not the transgressor," meaning that Allah hates sinners. Yet Jehovah God *loves* the sinner…the *exact opposite* of Allah! THANK

GOD!!! John 3:16, probably the most well-known verse in the entire world, proclaims: *"**For God so loved the world**, that he gave his only begotten Son, that whosoever believeth in him should not perish, but have everlasting life."* Romans 5:8 tells us, *"But God commendeth* [showed or demonstrated] *his love toward us,* **in that, while we were yet sinners,** *Christ died for us."* God Himself loved us so much He gave His very own life!

Besides this, there are many other differences between my God Jehovah and Allah, the so-called "god" of the fastest growing cult in the world. My God is a God of love—Allah is a god of murder. My God is a God of justice—Allah is a god of terror. My God is a God of peace—Allah is a god of war. My God is a God of joy and happiness—Allah is a god of hate and contentions. My God is a God of holiness and purity—Allah is a god who rewards his faithful servants with "heavenly" wickedness. My God is a God of Truth—Allah was dreamed up by the false prophet Muhammad. My God is a God of temperance (self-control)—Allah is a god of radical, murdering fanaticism. My God is the God of Christendom—Allah is the god of terrorist organizations, gangs, and rap singers. *My God does not slam jet liners loaded with innocent lives into buildings at a speed of over 300 mph!* My God doesn't destroy life; He creates it! My God is a God of creation, restoration, and preservation, not a "god" of devastation like Allah.

The books that claim to be God's Word and God inspired— the Book of Mormon and the Qur'an—contain corruptibility that our Jehovah God would *never* ordain. The Book of Mormon teaches the acceptance of polygamy [having many wives]. The Book of Mormon also teaches that God Himself was a polygamist, and these wives birthed Him many "spirit children" – you and me. Well, if this book that also claims to be inspired by God teaches the acceptance of polygamy, then why did God not create Adam with more than one wife? Just a thought-provoking question for you. The Qur'an teaches other corruptions along the same line, including polygamy, wife-beating, and the slaughtering of Jews and Christians.

As you can see, there is a difference *between all three books of "God."* Yet, if *God* has inspired *all **three*** then they would all be the same, because He is the same. Hebrews 13:8 says, *"Jesus Christ [is] the same yesterday, today, and forever."* Hebrews 1:12b says, *"thou art the same, and thy years shall not fail."* If God had written these three books then they would all say and teach the same things, NOT be different. God is not the author of confusion (I Corinthians 14:33), *Satan is.* God is not the father of lies, *Satan is! God is not corrupt with inconsistencies and inaccuracies and does not teach corrupt things;* **Satan is and does.**

The Bible *claims* to be inspired by God. There are powerful statements of this recorded in Scripture. The Word of God says in II Timothy 3:16, "All scripture is given *by inspiration of God."* II Peter 1:21 tells us, "For the prophecy came not in old time by the will of man: but holy men of God spake as they were *moved by the Holy Ghost."* II Samuel 23:1 relates, *"The Spirit of the LORD spake by me,* and *his word was in my tongue."* Ezra 1:1 states, *"…the word of the LORD by the mouth of Jeremiah…"* Acts 1:16 pronounces that *"this scripture…which the Holy Ghost by the mouth of David spake…"* The phrase *"Thus saith the LORD"* [or a similar phrase] has been stated **over 3,800 times** in just the *Old Testament alone!* So we can see that God definitely put the claim of inspiration on His Word.

It is common practice for an author to acknowledge his own book unless it was somehow proven that it was *not* written by that person. So when you look at the front of this book and see my name [Caleb M. Garraway] on the front of it, you automatically believe that I truly wrote this book and not somebody else. Well, then why don't we do the same thing with the Bible? *God* says that *He* wrote *His* Word, **so why don't we accept it as fact then?** What's the difference?

In the court of law, in order to say that "so-and-so" did not write a particular best-selling book, but you or somebody else actually did, you have **got** to have evidence (which is *not* based on thoughts, feelings, or emotion; but upon fact, documentation, and logistic proof) to even prove your point. So many are out there today trying to claim that God did not write the Bible, but **what proof** (I'm not talking about thoughts, feelings, or emotions) does the atheist, the liberal, the critical have to prove his point that God did *not* write it? I hear a lot of bad-mouthing, but I have never heard or seen any genuine proof yet.

History and Time Reveal It

Throughout the channels of history and the ages of time, the Bible over and over again proves that it is inspired by Jehovah God.

There has *always* been a crowd of people that have *always* questioned the Bible's historical accuracy. Nevertheless, the Bible has *always* come out true in the end, proving that God was right and men's criticism was wrong. Here are a few good examples out of many that we could discuss.

First of all—the existence of the Hittites civilization. Many times in Scripture the Bible makes reference to this society. In Exodus 33:2, the Bible says: *"And I will send an angel before thee; and I will drive out the Canaanite, the Amorite,* **and the Hittite***, and the Perizzite, the Hivite, and the Jebusite…"* Another reference to this ancient civilization is found in Deuteronomy 7:1 and 20:17. Deuteronomy 7:1 reads, *"When the LORD thy God shall bring thee into the land whither thou goest to possess it, and hath cast out many* **nations** *before thee,* **the Hittites***, and the Girgashites, and the Amorites, and the Canaanites, and the Perizzites, and the Hivites, and the Jebusites, seven* **nations** *greater and mightier than thou…"* Deuteronomy 20:17 says, *"But thou shalt utterly destroy them; namely, the Hittites, and the Amorites, the Canaanites, and the Perizzites, the Hivites, and the Jebusites; as the LORD thy God hath commanded thee…"* In Joshua 3:10, the Bible says, *"And Joshua said, Hereby ye shall know that the living God is among you, and that he will without fail drive out from before you the Canaanites, and* **the Hittites***, and the Hivites, and the Perizzites, and the Girgashites, and the Amorites, and the Jebusites."* Also, in Joshua 24:11, we find: *"And ye went over Jordan, and came unto Jericho: and the men of Jericho fought against you, the Amorites, and the Perizzites, and the Canaanites, and* **the Hittites***, and the Girgashites, the Hivites, and* *the Jebusites; and I delivered them into your hand."* The Bible tells us that Uriah, one of David's mightiest men of valor, was a Hittite. He was the husband of Bathsheba, with whom David committed adultery, and who was the mother of King Solomon.

Though the Word of God mentions the Hittites in many more portions of Scripture than what we have just read, the Hittite civilization remained archeologically hidden for centuries; therefore, historians labeled the Hittites to be a fabled society since no evidence had yet been discovered. Because the Bible contained a supposedly "fabled" society, many skeptics and critics used this as an excuse that the Bible was not true. Then in 1906, the Hittite civilization was discovered by archeological excavations about ninety miles east of Ankara, Turkey. There, the Hittites' last capitol which fell around 1200 B.C., was found.

Second—the evidence proving that the Flood actually took place. It is impossible to dismiss a world-wide Flood when there is so much evidence for it in history. I think of one of many of the scientific evidences—the jumbled animal burial grounds located all over the world…massive "graveyards" *full* of creatures suddenly buried and fossilized. The very existence of *single* fossils are evidence **enough** of a sudden burial by sediment and thick mud. The only way for a fossil to form is for the animal to be quickly buried before it can decay or its bones be scattered. Scientists have realized that *the only way* for fossilization to occur is by massive landslides, mud flows, volcanic eruptions, floods, or other natural disasters. I believe that each of those natural violent processes occurred in the worldwide Flood. Yes, *one* fossil is evidence of a great catastrophe, let alone large amounts of animals all jumbled violently together.

Near Agate Springs, Nebraska, there is a hill that contains approximately 9,000 closely packed animal fossils! Here, it seems that these animals (including rhinoceroses, camels, and giant boars) were trying to escape from something disastrous. This is not the only sight of this type of "graveyard." There is also another one of these places near Burgundy, France, on another hill over 1,000 feet above the surrounding plain. On a fissure, near the top of this hill is a crowded massive burial ground of fossils, animals that were quickly, suddenly, and violently buried; but *here* is one of most unusual things you will ever find. Here on this hill predators and preys were found fossilized **right alongside of each other!** Evidently, these animals were trying to avoid something disastrous, and the only major disaster that History shows to be that extreme is the Flood.

Not only are there a number of animal fossil "graveyards," but also there are a great number of ocean beds extending for *miles* full of fish fossils! Many of these beds, usually containing an estimated billion or more fish all jumbled together (definitely showing signs of a catastrophic upheaval), are found around the world in the different oceans. Today, it is very rare for a fish to be fossilized, let alone a whole school of them that extends for miles! The Bible teaches us that during the flood *"the fountains of the deep broke up"* (Genesis 7:11). This sudden upheaval captured a large of amount of marine life and buried them quickly, fossilizing them.

Third—the evidence in favor of Biblical creation rather than in favor of humanistic evolution, particularly the geologic column and transitional forms. Evolutionists say that the geologic column's rock layers of the earth should show the progression of life from the simplest fossil to the present day. The only problem with this is that evolutionists have not yet actually found this geologic column in one piece anywhere on earth like they have designed it in their textbooks.

Well, actually, I almost forgot; they supposedly *have* found the geologic column intact at the Grand Canyon. Supposedly, they found it on a cliff somewhere in the Canyon. They have a plaque there commemorating this site, distinguishing the different rock layers, and showing how it exactly fits the geologic column they have designed in their textbooks. *However,* the problem is that if you go around that *same* cliff to the other side of it, you will find *those **same** exact rock layers in a different order!* (What's going on with that?) The only place where you will find this supposed mythical geologic column is in a textbook. Evolutionists can't seem to find it any where else on earth no matter *how hard* they try.

Evolutionists are *always somehow* trying to turn away from evidence backing Biblical creation. Many desire to defy the presence of an "Higher Power" and the hand of Almighty God. But the fourth word of the Bible explains it all to us, *"In the beginning* **God** *created the heaven and the earth."* They say, "No, no. We have a 'Big Bang Theory.' That explains our creation and existence." Well, true; God said it, and BANG, it was there—*that* is the correct theory.

Evolutionists are trying to explain the evolution of man from the ape by different monkey-men species called "transitional forms." So I *do* want to ask—*Where are your transitional forms, Mr. Evolutionist?*

"Well," they reply, "one of our ancestors is the Piltdown man." Oh, yes, that's right…. But if I remember correctly, Mr. Piltdown man was made out of a chimpanzee's jawbone with a pig's tooth filed down and glued into place in the jaw! Then some "cohorts" and "professors" put the jawbone and tooth into chemicals to make it *look* old and real. And they came up with Mr. Piltdown. I'm sorry, but I don't think he really was a transition form after all.

Evolutionists hastily interject, "Well, then we have the Neanderthal man!" How could I forget about him? Are they talking about the same Neanderthal man that was found out to be after all just a human with inborn characteristics of severe arthritis and rickets, making him look like something between man and ape? That's right. They are. And there are many other "transitional form" scenarios just like these two. All turn out to be frauds.

Last of all—archaeological findings and historical documents *have confirmed* **the Biblical accuracy of names, dates and times, and places of many different kings and kingdoms.** For years, skeptics have questioned and doubted the existence of the Babylonian king Belshazzar that the Bible talks about in the book of Daniel. Belshazzar as king of the Babylonian empire was unknown, for there was no written history of his existence (besides the Bible, which skeptics and others *refuse* to accept as accurate history). Then in recent years, archeological discoveries proved his true existence just like the Bible said. While Belshazzar's father (Nabonidus, the real king of the Babylonian empire) was absent from Babylon, he left the rule of the kingdom in the hands of his son, Belshazzar. This explains why Belshazzar could only offer Daniel the position of *third in command* of the entire Babylonian kingdom (as talked about in Daniel 5:16 & 29), because King Nabonidus was first-in-command, Belshazzar second (although he assumed control of first-in-command during his father's absence), and Daniel third. In the end, the Bible was true after all. Men knew the truth for hundreds of years, but instead they decided to reject it until archeology proved to them what they would not believe from the Bible.

These four areas we've looked into are just a *scratch on the surface* of **many** examples of how the channels of history show the historical accuracy and prove the God-given inspiration of the Bible. Not only, though, is there evidence from the channels of history, but also there is evidence from the ages of time.

The ages of time show that the Bible is indestructible. Around A.D. 100 (after the book of Revelation was written by God through John), the Bible was finally complete after a span of 1,500 years of writing. God's completed Word did not just "fall off the scene" a few hundred years later or just become another old book that nobody was interested in any more. No, the Bible stood the test of time and has remained. God even promised this in the Bible. The Bible says in Isaiah 40:8: "The word of our God **shall** *stand for ever.*" Isaiah 55:11 says, "My word...**shall** *not return void.*" Isaiah 59:21 says, "My words...**shall** *not depart out of thy mouth.*" Jesus declared in Matthew 5:18, "One jot or one tittle **shall** *in no wise pass* from the law." Christ tells us in Matthew 24:35, "My words **shall not** *pass away.*" Again He says in Luke 16:17, "And it is easier for heaven and earth to pass, *than one tittle of the law* **to fail.**" It is easier for the universe *to be no more,* than the little mark in the letter "Q" to fail from being preserved in the Bible! The Word of God has **not** faded off the scene, but has stood time's test, continuing to be with us even today.

Many men have tried to tear down the Bible and its indestructibility, but the Word of God *still* remains and stands. In A.D. 303 Roman emperor Diocletian (A.D. 245-313) determined and decreed publicly that every Bible in his empire would be destroyed *under* **his** *hand.* He hated Christianity. He made this proclamation after one from his council told him that if he could destroy the Bible, then he would eliminate *Christianity* since Christians were people of the Bible. When he felt he had succeeded in completing this task, with devilish excitement Diocletian raised a monument baring an inscription in Latin: *"Extincto nomene Christianorum"*—"the name of Christianity is extinguished." But shortly after, Diocletian was replaced by Roman emperor Constantine. Less than ten years later, Diocletian's anti-Christian symbols were replaced with the symbol of the Cross. Under the reign of Constantine, Christians weren't persecuted as often as they were under the cruel rule of Diocletian, and their religious freedoms increased.

One renowned individual who loved mocking God and His Word was the French atheist Voltaire. One day he boasted foolishly *and* unwisely, "One hundred years from my day there will not be a Bible in the earth except one that is looked upon by an antiquarian curiosity seeker." Yet little did *he* know that twenty years after he died, the Geneva Bible Society would buy his house and use it as a *print shop to print the Word of God!* God *has* to have a sense of humor! A world-famous man challenges God and says that His Word is going to be gone in one hundred years. And in only 1/5 of that time (20 years), God is using *that man's very house* **as a print shop.** In addition, the Paris headquarters for the British Foreign Bible Society worked out of Voltaire's house. This society sent Bibles out *all over Europe.*

The Bible says in Galatians 6:7, "Be not deceived; **God is not mocked:** for whatsoever a man *soweth,* that **shall** he also reap." Every man will reap what he sows. Don't worry, the atheists and the liberals think they are getting away with cursing God now, but one day they **will** stand at the Great White Throne Judgment before the Almighty Heavenly Father and Jesus Christ and give account for every word and every deed.

God says in His Word that "the grass withereth, the flower fadeth: **but the word of our God shall stand for ever,**" that "the word of the Lord **endureth for ever**," and that "the Scripture **cannot** *be* **broken**." God is very emphatic about preserving His Word, and He will let *no one* stand in His way.

Fulfilled Prophecies Confirm It

All the fulfilled prophecies in the Bible *confirm* the fact that it **has** to be inspired of God. What other book in human existence has given several specific prophecies, and they all became fulfilled exactly as it was penned hundreds of years before? There is only **one** Book—God's Holy Word.

Let's *scratch the* **surface** of some of the many accurately fulfilled prophecies in the Bible. Several prophecies in the Old Testament dealt with the earthly life of Jesus Christ **alone**. Our Saviour fulfilled each of them while He lived on this earth.

Christ's virgin birth was prophesied in Isaiah 7:14, "Therefore the Lord himself shall give you a sign; Behold, *a **virgin** shall conceive,* and bear a son, and shall call his name *Immanuel*." This prophecy was fulfilled in the New Testament in Luke 1:26-35 and Matthew 1:18-25. The Bible says specifically in Luke 1:30-32 & 35, "30 And the angel said unto her, Fear not, Mary: for thou hast found favour with God. 31 And, behold, thou shalt conceive in thy womb, and bring forth a son, and shalt call his name JESUS. 32 He shall be great, and shall be called the Son of the Highest: and the Lord God shall give unto him the throne of his father David: 35 And the angel answered and said unto her, The Holy Ghost shall come upon thee, and the power of the Highest shall overshadow thee: therefore also that holy thing which shall be born of thee shall be called the Son of God." The Bible says in Matthew 1:20-25: "20 But while he thought on these things, behold, the angel of the Lord appeared unto him in a dream, saying, Joseph, thou son of David, fear not to take unto thee Mary thy wife: for that which is conceived in her is of the Holy Ghost. 21 And she shall bring forth a son, and thou shalt call his name JESUS: for he shall save his people from their sins. 22 *Now all this was done, that it might* be **fulfilled** *which was spoken of the Lord by the prophet,* saying, 23 Behold, *a **virgin** shall be with child,* and shall bring forth a son, and they shall call his name *Emmanuel,* which being interpreted is, God with us."

The Old Testament prophesies where Christ would be born in Micah 5:2, "But thou, Bethlehem Ephratah, though thou be little among the thousands of Judah, *yet out of **thee** shall **he** come forth* unto me that is to be ruler in Israel; whose goings forth have been from of old, from everlasting." And we can see that this prophecy has accurately been fulfilled in Luke 2:4-7, "4 And *Joseph also went up* from Galilee, out of the city of Nazareth, into Judaea, *unto the city of David, which is called **Bethlehem**;* (because he was of the house and lineage of David:) 5 To be taxed with Mary his espoused wife, being great with child. 6 And so it was, that, while they were there, the days were accomplished that she should be delivered. 7 *And she brought forth her firstborn son,* and wrapped him in swaddling clothes, and laid him in a manger; because there was no room for them in the inn."

In Isaiah 40:3, the Old Testament also talks about **the fore-coming of John the Baptist before Jesus Christ**: "*The voice of him that crieth in the wilderness,* Prepare ye the way of the LORD, make straight in the desert a highway for our God." In John 1:6-10, 15, 19-23, we can see this Old Testament prophecy fulfilled in the New Testament: "6 *There was a man sent from God, whose name was John.* 7 *The same came for a witness, to bear witness of the Light,* that all men through him might believe. 8 He was not that Light, but was sent to bear witness of that Light. 9 That was the true Light, which lighteth every man that cometh into the world. 10 He was in the world, and the world was made by him, and the world knew him not. 15 *John bare witness of him, and cried,* saying, This was he of whom I spake, He that cometh after me is preferred before me: for he was before me. 19 And this is the record of John, when the Jews sent priests and Levites from Jerusalem to ask him, *Who art thou?* 20 And he confessed, and denied not; but confessed, I am not the Christ. 21 And they asked him, What then? Art thou Elias? And he saith, *I am not.* Art thou that prophet? And he answered,

No. [22] Then said they unto him, **Who art thou?** that we may give an answer to them that sent us. What sayest thou of thyself? [23] He said, ***I am the voice of one crying in the wilderness***, *Make straight the way of the Lord, as said the prophet Esaias.*"

The Old Testament prophesies of **Christ's grand entrance into Jerusalem**, opening His passion week. It's even mentioned that Christ would ride on a donkey when He entered into the city. This is prophesied in the Old Testament in Zechariah 9:9: "Rejoice greatly, O daughter of Zion; shout, O daughter of Jerusalem: behold, *thy King cometh unto thee: he is just, and having salvation; lowly, and riding upon an ass,* and upon a colt the foal of an ass." And in Matthew 21:1-9 this *exact same thing* happened as Jesus entered the city. Notice what the Bible says in Matthew 21:1-9: "[1] And when they drew nigh unto Jerusalem, and were come to Bethphage, unto the mount of Olives, then sent Jesus two disciples, [2] Saying unto them, Go into the village over against you, and straightway ye shall find an ass tied, and a colt with her: loose them, and bring them unto me. [3] And if any man say ought unto you, ye shall say, The Lord hath need of them; and straightway he will send them. [4] All this was done, *that it might be fulfilled which was spoken by the prophet,* saying, [5] Tell ye the daughter of Sion, Behold, thy King cometh unto thee, meek, and sitting upon an ass, and a colt the foal of an ass. [6] And the disciples went, and did as Jesus commanded them, [7] And brought the ass, and the colt, and put on them their clothes, and they set him thereon. [8] And a very great multitude spread their garments in the way; others cut down branches from the trees, and strawed them in the way. [9] And the multitudes that went before, and that followed, cried, saying, Hosanna to the Son of David: Blessed is he that cometh in the name of the Lord; Hosanna in the highest."

The most fascinating of the Old Testament prophecies about the life of Jesus Christ are those concerning His death on the cross and the events taking place while He was dying. One thing that is interesting is that when these prophecies were penned, crucifixion was a method of execution that *was not even heard of.* Crucifixion was a *Roman* form of punishment, *not* a Jewish one.

Therefore, the prophets of God who prophesied Christ's death by crucifixion were **oblivious** to this type of execution. Nevertheless, the Old Testament, many hundreds of years prior, prophesied *accurately* what happened. Let's take a look at *eight prophecies* in particular.

One, Christ's hands and feet were pierced. Psalms 22 is a passage reflecting Christ's death on the cross. Psalms 22:16 says: "For dogs have compassed me: the assembly of the wicked have inclosed me: *they pierced my hands and my feet.*" This was fulfilled at the cross, but more specifically we can read both John 20:24-29 and Luke 24:39-40. John 20:24-29 says, "24 But Thomas, one of the twelve, called Didymus, was not with them when Jesus came. 25 The other disciples therefore said unto him, We have seen the Lord. But he said unto them, Except I shall see in his hands the print of the nails, and put my finger into *the print of the nails*, and thrust my hand into his side, I will not believe. 26 And after eight days again his disciples were within, and Thomas with them: then came Jesus, the doors being shut, and stood in the midst, and said, Peace be unto you. 27 Then saith he to Thomas, *Reach hither thy finger, and behold my hands*; and reach hither thy hand, and thrust it into my side: and be not faithless, but believing. 28 And Thomas answered and said unto him, My Lord and my God. 29 Jesus saith unto him, Thomas, because thou hast seen me, thou hast believed: blessed are they that have not seen, and yet have believed." Luke 24:39-40 says, "39 Behold *my hands and my feet*, that it is I myself: handle me, and see; for a spirit hath not flesh and bones, as ye see me have. 40 And when he had thus spoken, *he shewed them his hands and his feet.*"

Two, Christ was mocked upon the Cross. This is prophesied in the Old Testament in Psalms 22:6-8: "6 But I am a worm, and no man; a reproach of men, and despised of the people. 7 All they that see me laugh me to scorn: they shoot out the lip, they shake the head, saying, 8 He trusted on the LORD that he would deliver him: let him deliver him, seeing he delighted in him." And we can see from Scripture in the New Testament in Mark 15:29-32 (as well as in the other Gospels) that the Pharisees and others jeered and mocked Christ as He hung on the Cross. Mark 15 says, "*29* And they that passed by *railed on him, wagging their heads*, and saying, Ah, thou that destroyest the temple, and buildest it in three days, *30* Save thyself, and come down from the cross. *31* Likewise also the chief priests ***mocking*** said among themselves with the scribes, He saved others; himself he cannot save. *32* Let Christ the King of Israel descend now from the cross, that we may see and believe. And they that were crucified with him *reviled* him."

Three, as Christ hung on the Cross, darkness came. Psalms 22:2 prophesies this: "O my God, I cry in the daytime, but thou hearest not; and *in the night season*, and am not silent." I also find it interesting that in Amos 8:9, the Old Testament says, "And it shall come to pass in that day, saith the Lord GOD, that I will cause the sun to go down at **noon**, and I will darken the earth in the clear day." Now notice what the New Testament has to say in Matthew 27:45: "Now from *the **sixth** hour* there was darkness over all the land unto the ninth hour." The sixth hour in Jewish time is about our 12 PM. In Amos it says that the sun went down at *noon* or around the sixth hour!

Four, Christ was given vinegar to drink while on the Cross. The Old Testament prophesies this in Psalms 69:21: "They gave me also *gall* for my meat; and in my thirst *they gave me vinegar to drink.*" Matthew 27:34 & 48 shows the fulfillment of this prophecy (as well as in Mark 15:23 and John 19:28-30). Matthew 27:34 & 48 say, "*34* They gave him *vinegar to drink* mingled *with gall:* and when he had tasted thereof, he would not drink. *48* And straightway one of them ran, and took a sponge, and filled it *with vinegar*, and put it on a reed, and gave him to drink."

Five, the Roman soldiers were casting lots for Christ's garments. Psalms 22:18 prophesies, "They *part my garments* among them, and *cast lots* **upon** my vesture." John 19:23-24 *clearly* shows how this prophecy is *accurately* fulfilled. The Bible says there, "*23* Then the soldiers, when they had crucified Jesus, *took his garments, and made four parts, to every soldier a part;* and also his coat: now the coat was without seam, woven from the top throughout. *24* They said therefore among themselves, Let us not rend it, *but cast* *lots for it*, whose it shall be: ***that the scripture might be fulfilled***, which saith, They parted my raiment among them, and for my vesture they did cast lots. These things therefore the soldiers did." Mark 15:24 also says, "And when they had crucified him, they *parted his garments, casting lots* **upon** them, what every man should take."

Six, throughout the entire crucifixion not one bone was broken in His entire body. Amazing, this specific fact is very accurately prophesied in Psalms 34:20: "He keepeth *all* his bones: *not one* of them is broken." Approximately 1000 years later in John 19:32-33 & 36, the New Testament reveals to us: "32 Then came the soldiers, and brake the legs of the first, and of the other which was crucified with him. 33 But when they came to Jesus, and saw that he was dead already, they brake **not** his legs: 36 For these things were done, *that the scripture should be fulfilled*, A bone of him shall not be broken."

Seven, Christ cried out, "My God, my God, why hast thou forsaken me?" Psalms 22:1 says, *"My God, my God, why hast thou forsaken me? why art thou so far from helping me, and from the words of my roaring?"* And Christ said those *very same* **words** on the Cross at Calvary. Mark 15:34 (as well as Matthew 27:46) reveals: "And at the ninth hour Jesus cried with a loud voice, saying, Eloi, Eloi, lama sabachthani? which is, being interpreted, *My God, my God, why hast thou forsaken me?*" – Christ's fulfillment of that very same prophecy.

Think with me for a brief moment and with your mind's eye glimpse what it must have been like for our Christ. *Consider* what He went through in agony and suffering and pain in order for us to be saved, in order for us to go out and tell lost souls of His salvation plan! Beaten to a bloody pulp, disfigured, marred horrendously, and unrecognizable, He became vile sin and pure evil *for us*. No longer was His Father or heaven cheering Him on, but He was *forsaken* and by Himself. As He *saw* the skies blacken and the Celestial doors shut because He was taking upon Himself the blackest of sins, He frantically screamed out on the Cross: "Eli! *Eli!!!* Lama sabachthani?!?" ***"DADDY!!!!*** Where are You? It's dark!

I'm lonely! **DADDY!!!!** *Why hast Thou forsaken Me????"* Yet after an intense struggle against sin and Satan, Messiah Jesus was able to *crush* that Serpent's head and quickly and loudly cried out to His Father and the heavenly host… **"IT IS FINISHED!** *The victory's won!"*

Eight, Christ's side was pierced. Zechariah 12:10 states, "And I will pour upon the house of David, and upon the inhabitants of Jerusalem, the spirit of grace and of supplications: *and they shall look upon me **whom they have pierced,** and they shall mourn for him, as one mourneth for his only son, and shall be in bitterness for him, as one that is in bitterness for his firstborn." In John 19:33-35 & 37, this prophecy was fulfilled: "[33] But when they came to Jesus, and saw that he was dead already, they brake not his legs: [34] But one of the soldiers *with a spear **pierced** his side,* and forthwith came there out blood and water. [35] And he that saw it bare record, and his record is true: and he knoweth that he saith true, that ye might believe. [37] And again another scripture saith, They shall look on him whom they pierced."

Now, from a logical perspective, what do you think the probability or chances are for someone to fulfill just the eight prophecies that we looked at involving Calvary? My 10th grade Bible teacher told my class one day after teaching various prophecies fulfilled by Christ, "The chance that any man might have lived to fulfill all eight prophecies of Christ is one in 100 quadrillion (a one with seventeen zeros after it)!" To illustrate this point, he continued, "Let's say we took silver dollars and covered the state of Texas with them until it was two feet deep. Now if we marked one of these silver dollars and put it somewhere in Texas, and then blindfolded you and told you that you had to pick that marked silver dollar to win the prize, what are the chances that you would pick it? The same chance that the prophets would have of writing just eight of these prophecies and having them all come true for any one man if they had written them without God's inspiration!" *(Statistic from the calculations of Christian author and speaker Josh McDowell)*

So we can see that the events around Calvary were not only prophesied hundreds of years before the actual crucifixion, but they were also *accurately* fulfilled and recorded in the New Testament. Are these the *only* prophecies about Christ that were fulfilled? No. There are **over 300 additional prophecies** that Christ fulfilled! That's quite impressive. Let's take a look at a few more prophecies Christ fulfilled to even more prove the point.

In Isaiah 53:9, the Old Testament prophesied that **Jesus would be laid in a rich man's tomb**: "And he made his grave with the wicked, and *with the rich in his death;* because he had done no violence, neither was any deceit in his mouth." And in the New Testament recorded in Matthew 27:57-60: "⁵⁷ When the even was come, there came *a rich man* of Arimathaea, named Joseph, who also himself was Jesus' disciple: ⁵⁸ He went to Pilate, and begged the body of Jesus. Then Pilate commanded the body to be delivered. ⁵⁹ And when Joseph had taken the body, he wrapped it in a clean linen cloth, ⁶⁰ And laid it in his own new tomb, which he had hewn out in the rock: and he rolled a great stone to the door of the sepulchre, and departed."

The Old Testament also prophesies **Christ's resurrection**. Psalms 16:10 says, "For thou wilt not leave my soul in Hell; *neither wilt thou suffer thine Holy One to see corruption.*" "Thine Holy One" is Jesus Christ. It is also interesting to note that Jesus Christ *Himself* told what would happen. He even gave a sign in Matthew 12:40, "For as Jonas was three days and three nights in the whale's belly; *so shall the Son of man be three days and three nights in the heart of the earth.*" In John 2:19, speaking of Himself, Jesus said to others, "Destroy this temple, and *in three days I will raise it up.*" Over and over again Jesus told His disciples that He would rise again on the third day. Matthew 16:21 tells us, "From that time forth began Jesus to shew unto his disciples, how that he must go unto Jerusalem, and suffer many things of the elders and chief priests and scribes, and be killed, and *be raised again **the third day**.*" We can see at the end of each of the four Gospels that Christ rose again on the third day. Hallelujah! What a Saviour.

I just want to show you what one of the Gospels has to say about Christ's resurrection; Matthew 28:1-10 relates to us: *"¹ In the end of the sabbath, as it began to dawn toward the first day of the week, came Mary Magdalene and the other Mary to see the sepulchre. ² And, behold, there was a great earthquake: for the angel of the Lord descended from heaven, and came and rolled back the stone from the door, and sat upon it. ³ His countenance was like lightning, and his raiment white as snow: ⁴ And for fear of him the keepers did shake, and became as dead men. ⁵ And the angel answered and said unto the women, Fear not ye: for I know that ye seek Jesus, which was crucified. ⁶ He is not here: for he is risen, as he said. Come, see the place where the Lord lay. ⁷ And go quickly, and tell his disciples that he is risen from the dead; and, behold, he goeth before you into Galilee; there shall ye see him: lo, I have told you. ⁸ And they departed quickly from the sepulchre with fear and great joy; and did run to bring his disciples word. ⁹ And as they went to tell his disciples, behold, Jesus met them, saying, All hail. And they came and held him by the feet, and worshipped him. ¹⁰ Then said Jesus unto them, Be not afraid: go tell my brethren that they go into Galilee, and there shall they see me."*

Can't you see what might have happened *before* that stone was rolled away from the tomb face? It had to be a very dramatic moment. Satan and his hosts were probably working their best to keep Jesus held down...to not come back to life. Can't you see it now? On that third day, Jesus' body started wiggling on the tomb bed around which the demons had been delightfully dancing in triumph the night before. Then Death and Sin cried out as they began to lose their grip on the body of King Jesus! So Allah, Buddha, Maroni, Brahma, Confusius, and all the various false prophets and deities jumped over and tried to keep Him held down while Satan shouted over their shoulders, "You've got to keep Him down... DON'T LET HIM ARISE!" But praise His name – *up from the grave He arose* with a *mighty triumph* o'er His foes! He arose a Victor that day, on Sunday, over the Dark Domain; and He lives *forever* with His saints to reign! Paul tells us in I Corinthians 15:4, "And that he was buried, and that he rose again *the third day according to the scriptures.*"

The Old Testament also prophecies of **Jesus ascending back into heaven**. Psalms 110:1 says, "The LORD said unto my Lord, *Sit thou at my right hand,* until I make thine enemies thy footstool." And that is exactly what Jesus is doing today. He is sitting at the right hand of the throne of the Father. Hebrews 1:3 says: "Who being the brightness of his glory, and the express image of his person, and upholding all things by the word of his power, when he had by himself purged our sins, *sat down **on the right hand** of the Majesty* on high." Furthermore, Ephesians 1:20 announces, "Which he wrought in Christ, *when he raised him from the dead,* and set him at *his own right hand* in the heavenly places." Hebrews 12:2 says, "Looking unto Jesus the author and finisher of our faith; who for the joy that was set before him endured the cross, despising the shame, *and is set down at the right hand of the throne of God.*"

I find it interesting that Psalms 24:3-10 and Acts 1:9-11 correlate. Psalms 24:3-10 speaks of the King of glory, the LORD of hosts, ascending into heaven. And in Acts 1:9-11 Jesus ascends right up to heaven just as He finished talking to His eleven beloved disciples. Psalms 24:3-10 says, "3 Who *shall ascend* into the hill of the LORD [Zion]? or who shall stand in his holy place? 4 He that hath clean hands, and a pure heart; who hath not lifted up his soul unto vanity, nor sworn deceitfully. 5 He shall receive the blessing from the LORD, and righteousness from the God of his salvation. 6 This is the generation of them that seek him, that seek thy face, O Jacob. Selah. 7 Lift up your heads, O ye gates; and be ye lift up, ye everlasting doors; and the King of glory shall come in. 8 Who is this King of glory? The LORD strong and mighty, the LORD mighty in battle. 9 Lift up your heads, O ye gates; even lift them up, ye everlasting doors; and the King of glory shall come in. 10 Who is this King of glory? The LORD of hosts, he is the King of glory." Now compare this to Acts 1:9-11: "9 And when he had spoken these things, while they beheld, *he was taken up;* and a cloud received him out of their sight. 10 And while they looked stedfastly toward heaven as he went up, behold, two men stood by them in white apparel; 11 Which also said, Ye men of Galilee, why stand ye gazing up into heaven? this same Jesus, *which is taken up from you into heaven*, shall so come in like manner as ye have seen him go into heaven."

There are many prophecies in the Bible about Jesus Christ that have been fulfilled *accurately* in the New Testament during His earthly life. We have only glimpsed some of the numerous prophecies about our Lord. There are so many Old Testament prophecies in general that have been fulfilled in the New Testament that we could write volumes about them. Here is another "handful" of them just to prove the point.

PROPHECY OF CHRIST	OLD TESTAMENT REFERENCES	NEW TESTAMENT REFERENCES
Be adored by great persons	*Psalms 72:10-11*	*Matthew 2:1-11*
Be anointed with the Spirit of God	*Isaiah 11:2, 61:1*	*Matthew 3:16; John 3:34; Acts 10:38*
Be hated without cause	*Isaiah 49:7; Psalms 69:4*	*John 15:24-25*
Be undesired and rejected by His own people	*Isaiah 53:2, 63:3; Psalms 69:8*	*Mark 6:3; Luke 9:58; John 1:11,*
Be plotted against by Jews & Gentiles	*Psalms 2:1-2*	*Acts 4:27*
Be betrayed by a friend	*Psalms 41:9, 55:12-24*	*Matthew 26:21-25, 47-50; John 13:18-21; Acts 1:16-18*
Be betrayed for 30 pieces of silver	*Zechariah 11:12*	*Matthew 26:16*
Have his price given for a potter's field	*Zechariah 11:13*	*Matthew 27:7*
Be forsaken by His disciples	*Zechariah 13:7*	*Matthew 26:31, 56*
Be struck on the cheek	*Micah 5:1*	*Matthew 27:30*
Be spat on	*Isaiah 50:6*	*Matthew 26:67; 27:30*
Be mocked	*Psalms 22:7-8*	*Matthew 27:31, 39-44*
Be beaten	*Isaiah 50:6*	*Matthew 26:67; 27:26, 30*

PROPHECY OF CHRIST	OLD TESTAMENT REFERENCES	NEW TESTAMENT REFERENCES
Be thirsty during His execution	*Psalms 22:15*	*John 19:28*
Be given vinegar to quench that thirst	*Psalms 69:21*	*Matthew 27:34*
Be sought after by Gentiles as well as Jews	*Isaiah 11:10; 42:1*	*Acts 10:45*
Be accepted by the Gentiles	*Isaiah 11:10; 42:1-4, 49:1-12*	*Matthew 12:21; Romans 15:9-12*

Beyond a shadow of a doubt we can see that the fulfilled prophecies of the Word of God are one of the proofs *why* the Bible is truly inspired of God. If *men* had written the Bible, how could they have possibly known what would happen hundreds of years after them? How could they have accurately prophesied what would one day happen? *...over 300 wonderful details...* Moreover, how would they even know when Christ would come, let alone how and where? Thus, our Bible *has* to be the inspired Word of God.

SCIENCE AGREES WITH IT

Sir William Herschel (classical composer & astronomer who discovered Uranus and infrared radiation) once said: *"All human discoveries seem to be made only for the purpose of confirming more strongly the truths contained in the Holy Scriptures."* There are **several** scientific facts the Bible taught long before man realized they actually existed. When they were "discovered" to be true, it just proved *again* how the Word of God is accurate and **had** to be from the breath of God.

1. The Bible discusses *the circulation of the atmosphere*. Ecclesiastes 1:6 reveals this fact: "The wind goeth toward the south, and turneth about unto the north; it whirleth about

continually, and the wind returneth again *according to his circuits*." Hundreds of years later, scientists have discovered that there are six wind patterns that surround the earth and continue to rotate like a track.

2. The Bible talks about **the atmosphere protecting us from outside harm**. This can be found in Isaiah 40:22, which says: "It is he [God]…that stretcheth out *the heavens* as **a curtain**, and spreadeth them out *as a **tent*** to dwell in." This word "heavens" used here in Isaiah 40:22 means "sky" in the Hebrew. Therefore, the Bible is telling us that the "sky" is stretched out as a curtain; and if you think of it, a curtain pulled in front of a window *blocks*, *shades,* and *protects* from the sun and other outside elements. The "sky," the Bible says, is spread out as a tent. Again, this gives us the sense of protection or being sheltered. A tent is something you sleep in when you are outdoors; it keeps you *protected* from outside elements and harm. This is true with our atmosphere. Our atmosphere is our protection from outer and harm, such as UV radiation, meteors, and other space elements.

3. The Bible speaks of **the water cycle in the atmosphere**. In Ecclesiastes 1:7 the Bible says, "All the rivers run into the sea; yet the sea is not full; unto the place from whence the rivers come, *thither they return again*." The Bible delves deeper and very specifically discusses each of the water cycle "steps" you learn about in school: evaporation, condensation, and precipitation. Briefly allow me to give you a "sketchy" overview of these processes in the atmospheric water cycle. The atmospheric water cycle begins with evaporation, when water evaporates into the air. Then this evaporated water slowly rises high up into the atmosphere to condense or "melt together" on dust particles to form little droplets of water. This process of condensation is what forms the "white puffiness" of the clouds – millions of little water droplets. These little water droplets continue to merge into other droplets to make

bigger drops. Then when these drops are too heavy to float in the air, they fall back down to the ground in the form of rain —precipitation. Then the water eventually runs back down into the oceans as the Bible says, and the process starts all over again. Psalms 135:7 and Jeremiah 10:13 both speak about evaporation. Psalms 135:7 says, "He causeth the vapours to ascend from the ends of the earth." And Jeremiah 10:13 says, "He causeth the vapours to ascend from the ends of the earth." The Bible also specifically speaks on condensation in Job 26:8 and Job 36:27a. Job 26:8 says, "He bindeth up the waters in his thick clouds; and the cloud is not rent under them." Job 36:27a says, "For he maketh small the drops of water." And in Job 36:27b and 28, God in His Word speaks of precipitation: "27b they pour down rain according to the vapour thereof: 28 Which the clouds do drop and distil upon man abundantly." Man did not "discover" the atmospheric water cycle and its distinct processes until thousands of years later. This shows once again that the Bible is accurate *again* in the field of science, proving its God-given inspiration.

4. The Bible taught long before man realized it that **the atmosphere has a weight to it**. It was not until the seventeenth century that Galileo and his student Torricelli discovered this fact, yet the Bible talked about it thousands of years prior in Job 28:25: "To make *the weight for the winds; and he weigheth the waters by measure.*" This verse and the preceding verses tell us that God made *weight* for the *winds*. Through experimentation, we have been able to calculate that the air at sea level weighs 14.7 pounds per square inch. That means if you have an average 3' x 4' desk, there is an incredible weight of about 2,117 pounds of force pushing down on top of the desk! That's over a ton of weight!

5. The Bible spoke about **the law of gravity** in Job 38:6 thousands of years before the apple supposedly fell on Sir Isaac Newton's head leading him to "discover" the law of gravity

after experimentation. The Bible rhetorically questioned in Job 38:6, "Whereupon are *the foundations* thereof *fastened?*" or "How or by what is the earth kept as a sphere?" The question was given for man to find out. Science now shows through credible data that *gravity* keeps the earth a sphere.

6. In Leviticus 17:11, the Bible talks about **blood circulation** and that **the blood of the body sustains our life**. Leviticus 17:11 says, "For the life of the flesh is in the blood." *This* scientific fact was not even discovered in the days of George Washington! If the physicians had known it, then they would not have put leeches on him to get rid of his "bad blood." Since they did not know it, the life of one of America's greatest heroes, George Washington, was shortened by this unscientific practice. William Thayer says in his excellent biography of George Washington, "*Sixty years later* it [the process of bleeding] was still in use, and no one can doubt it deprived [him] of his chance of living. The irony of the whole account was that beside his bed that day was a copy of the Bible. In that Bible could be found Leviticus 17:11—'For the life of the flesh is in the blood.'" In the 1800's, man finally discovered that this process of "bleeding" or "blood letting" was unscientific, for it was discovered (just as the Bible had said) that blood *did* sustain life.

7. The Bible teaches that **man's body and the earth are of the same chemical composition**. We can see this in Psalms 103:14 and Genesis 3:19. Psalms 103:14 says, "For he knoweth our frame; he remembereth that *we are dust*." In Genesis 2:7, the Bible gives the story of how God created man... with the dust of the ground, from the earth. It says there: "And the LORD God formed man *of the dust of the ground,* and breathed into his nostrils the breath of life; and man became a living soul." In Genesis 3:19, God reminds man that he was made of the earth. Genesis 3:19 says, "In the sweat of thy face shalt thou eat bread, till thou return unto

the ground; for *out of it wast thou taken: for dust thou art, and unto dust shalt thou return.*" We are nothing more than dirt from the earth! This scientific fact, which the Bible talked about in the first book of the Bible, was not "discovered" by man until thousands of years later because of a lack of technological advancements and Biblical knowledge.

8. The Bible speaks of **the earth being suspended in space**. Job 26:7 says, "He...hangeth the earth upon *nothing.*" Not until the Middle Ages with the invention of the telescope was this fact noted by man to be truly scientific.

9. The Bible also showed to us thousands of years ago that **the earth rotates on an axis**. Ecclesiastes 1:5 most clearly addresses this subject, saying, "The sun also ariseth, and the sun goeth down, and hasteth to his place where he arose." Not only does this verse signify the rotation of the earth, but it also implicates the earth's rotation in relation to the sun. This fact that the earth revolved around the sun was counted as heresy by the Roman Catholic Church, but as the use of telescopes became more prevalent among scientists, the truth from the Bible became accepted as more scientists began to declare its accuracy.

10. The Bible teaches that **the earth is round**. The Bible claims this scientific fact in Isaiah 40:22, saying: "It is he that sitteth upon *the circle of the earth.*" For many thousands of years—even in the days of Christopher Columbus—many believed the earth was flat. It is said that Christopher Columbus stumbled across this verse in Scripture and, therefore, *believed* this fact to be true, because the Bible had said it. So, in wanting to reach the East Indies, Columbus realized that if he just sailed west, he would soon reach the East Indies in the East. Yet little did he know that he had something blocking his way, and it was the New World— the Western Hemisphere. Hence, Columbus became the

first famous discoverer of the Americas because he read and believed this verse of Scripture in his Bible one day. After a while, men began to venture out into the unknown of the seas, and Ferdinand Magellan and his crew became the first people to sail around the world, proving once and for all that the earth was definitely round just as the Bible had claimed for thousands of years!

11. The Bible says that **the stars are a huge distance from the earth**. Job 22:12 tells us this: "Behold the height of the stars, how high they are!" The sun in our solar system is the closest star to earth, yet the sun is *93,000,000* miles away! Think of it this way; if you were to drive that distance non-stop in a car going the speed limit at 70 mph, it would take you approximately 1,328,571 hours to drive that distance! In other words, you would be driving about 55,357 days or 151½ *years* to get to the sun! That's a long time. The second closest star to planet Earth is *Proxima Centauri*, which is about 25,000,000,000,000 [25 trillion] miles away! Just think how long it would take to get to *that* star if you drove the speed limit [approximately 7,134,703 years]! Yes, I believe that the Bible is quite accurate when it says, "Behold the height of the stars, how high they are!"

12. The Bible teaches that **the stars are innumerable**. Jeremiah 33:22 says, "…the host of heaven cannot be numbered…" Yet, man in his stubbornness has tried to count all the stars that he could see. First, a fellow named Hipparchus in 130 B.C. counted 1,022 stars in the sky. Then Ptolemy in A.D. 200 counted 1,026 stars. *Now* man has built powerful telescopes and has even launched some into space so he can see farther into the universe. Men have tried to count all the stars that they could see, but they have now given up, saying that is *impossible* to count all the stars in the heavens! Funny, right? In the end, man finally gives in and agrees with what the Bible has to say in Jeremiah 33:22.

13. The Bible states that ***the stars differ in magnitude***. Around 2,000 years ago, I Corinthians 15:41 was written and says: "There is one glory of the sun, and another glory of the moon, and another glory of the stars: *for one star differeth from another star in glory.*" And now today with the help of telescopes, man has realized that stars differ in their magnitude [size and brightness], as the Bible says. They have even made classification for different types of stars out there, from the least to the greatest, by their color.

14. The Bible has revealed for thousands of years that ***stars travel in orbits***. Judges 5:20 says, "They fought from heaven; *the stars in their **courses** fought against Sisera.*" Many "scientists" scoffed at this verse because from a regular point of view from the earth with your eyes, the stars seem motionless, just twinkling in the heavens. After the invention of the telescope scoffers had to silence themselves, for it was true. Stars traveled in orbital routes.

15. The Bible teaches that ***the universe is immeasurable***. The Bible speaks of this in Jeremiah 31:37: "Thus saith the LORD; *If heaven above can be measured,* and the foundations of the earth searched out beneath, I will also cast off all the seed of Israel for all that they have done, saith the LORD." God made a covenant with Abraham, Isaac, and Jacob that he would make their seed as the sands of the sea (uncountable). The children of Israel are God's chosen people, and God cannot "cast off all the seed of Israel" because He has made a covenant, and God will *always* keep His word. Therefore, we can infer from this verse that the universe cannot be measured because if it *could* be measured, God would have to cast off all the seed of Israel, which He has given His word of oath never to do. Yet despite what the Bible says, scientists *even today* still want to waste their time trying to measure the universe, even though God said that it was impossible. (Briefly, I also want to expound upon the part of Jeremiah

31:37 that says: "If...*the foundations of the earth* [can be] *searched out,* I will also cast off all the seed of Israel..." God says that if we could search the foundations—or the center— of the earth, He would cast out all of Israel. Well, we have already mentioned that God will never cast out all of Israel because of His covenant; *therefore*, we cannot search the "center" of the earth! So the book *Journey to the Center of the Earth* by Jules Verne may be an excellent fictional classic, but Biblically it is heretical, *because God cannot go against His Word that He has given.*)

16. The Bible says that **the Universe is running down**. This is the second law of thermodynamics that man finally "discovered" in the past few hundred years. This second law, known as entropy, says that everything in the universe has a tendency to go from order to disorder. The Bible originally taught the second law of thermodynamics in Psalms 102:25-26, saying, "25 Of old hast thou laid the foundation of the earth: and the heavens are the work of thy hands. 26 *They shall perish*, but thou shalt endure: yea, *all of them shall wax old like a garment*; as a vesture shalt thou change them, and they shall be changed."

17. The Bible gives the explanation for something that scientists have called *the strong nuclear force*. Scientists have not actually found out what this strong nuclear force is, but *we* can understand what it is, because the Bible talks about it. Before we look at these verses, let me give a brief explanation. Scientists have discovered within the nucleus of every atom that there are protons and neutrons. Protons are positive, and neutrons are neutral in charge. The nature of protons is to repel from each other as far as they can, as quickly as possible. They push away at each other with a force of 560,000 pounds, yet in the nucleus they cling together as if they were bound. Scientist *then* discovered the reason for this phenomenon. They found **another** force working in the atom pushing those

protons together with a force of 560,000,000 pounds…1000 times greater than the force with which protons repel each other. They nicknamed this mysterious power the *"strong nuclear force."* But I believe it is something else! Look at what the Bible says in Colossians 1:16-17: "For by him (Who? King Jesus.) were all things created, that are in heaven, and that are in earth, visible and invisible, whether they be thrones, or dominions, or principalities, or powers: *all things were created by him and for him:* And he is before all things, *and by him all things* **consist**." By **Christ** all things consist and are "held together." He is the One who holds the very protons in the nucleus of all the atoms of the world together. I say that *the strong nuclear force* is the hand of King Jesus.

These seventeen scientific facts (although there are many more) mentioned in the Bible thousands of years before man actually "discovered" them are one of the proofs why the Bible was written by God. If mere men had written the Bible, then we would have already known these scientific facts long before these past few hundred years. As originally stated, what Sir William Herschel said sums it all up: *"All human discoveries seem to be made only for the purpose of confirming more strongly the truths contained in the Holy Scripture."* My friend, science agrees with the fact that the Bible has been inspired of God!

ITS CHANGING OF LIVES MAKES YOU BELIEVE IT

One of the most convincing proofs that *confirm* the Bible as God's inspired Word is that it changes lives.

Think of the maniac of Gadara, and who *he* was. He was a wild, demon-possessed man that cut himself with sharp rocks and ran crazily through the tombs (a nude dude in a rude mood)! … Then Jesus passed by… Oh, how this man's life was transformed by the **words** of God! Jesus commanded the devils to come out of the man, and a little while later, the Bible says this same "maniac" was sitting by the side of the road, clothed, and in his *right* mind. All because of the Word of God.

Think of Paul, who was first called Saul. He was a murderer of Christians. Just think of all the Christians that he and his band dragged off to prison to be killed. All the midnight raids that he was the mastermind behind…beating and killing men, dragging off women and children in shackles, throwing them into dungeons. In I Timothy 1:12-15, Paul gives a summary of his testimony: "12 And I thank Christ Jesus our Lord, who hath enabled me, for that he counted me faithful, putting me into the ministry; 13 Who was before *a blasphemer, and a persecutor, and injurious:* but I obtained mercy, because I did it ignorantly in unbelief. 14 And the grace of our Lord was exceeding abundant with faith and love which is in Christ Jesus. 15 This is a faithful saying, and worthy of all acceptation, that Christ Jesus came into the world to save sinners; *of whom I am chief.*" How was his life changed? By the Word of God. You could spend a lifetime listening to story after story of how the Bible has changed the lives of people. There are testimonies upon testimonies of men and women who lived a life of sin in drugs, alcohol, and promiscuity. Maybe some of your own parents, like mine, were saved later in life and came out of that mess. Then when they had gotten saved, their lives were turned around and were completely changed. How did it happen? Was it through Alcoholics Anonymous? Was it through Drug Rehab? No. *It was through the Word of God.* It was *salvation* by the convicting power of the Word of God through the Holy Spirit.

Psalms 119:9 says, "Wherewithal shall a young man cleanse his way? by taking heed thereto *according to **thy word*** [God's Word]." Jeremiah 23:29 also says, "Is not my word like as *a fire?* saith the LORD; and like *a hammer that breaketh the rock in pieces?*" This definitely shows that the Word of God has power to it and that it has power like fire and a hammer to transform the lives of individuals!

There are many pastors and men in the ministry today that lived a former life of a druggie, hippie, bar bouncer, and you name it!

I think of Sam Jones, a successful lawyer yet a heavy alcoholic. What happened to him? He got saved, and the powerful Word of God changed his life. He became a flaming, leather-lunged evangelist, and by the end of his lifetime he was known as "The Moody of the South."

I think of Billy Sunday, a great professional baseball player, yet he too was a heavy drinker. Then one night he decided to give up his sinful lifestyle, and he stumbled into the Pacific Garden Mission in Chicago and got saved! The powerful Word of God changed his life completely, and he *On Calvary* became one of the greatest evangelists this world has ever known. He's given several soul-stirring statements such as: *"Let's quit fiddling with religion and do something to bring the world to Christ."* And, *"I'll keep preaching till Hell freezes over."*

There are *so many other stories* of individuals getting saved by the Word of God and their lives forever being changed. No, they did not become world famous, but they certainly became great servants for God.

I think of William R. Newell, a pastor's son who was in deep spiritual darkness and believed himself to be possessed of the Devil as Judas Iscariot, to have committed the unpardonable sin, and to be forever unable to be saved. Reluctantly, R. A. Torrey brought Newell to the Moody Bible Institute under guard after receiving many brokenhearted letters from Newell's father and his father's friends. One day Torrey brought this young man into his superintendent's office and began quoting Scripture—mainly John 6:37 where Jesus Christ says, *"Him that cometh to me I will in no wise cast out,"* challenging him to be saved before it was too late. After some length of time, the Word of God finally softened Newell's heart and put him under Holy Spirit conviction. Moments after, R. A. Torrey was able to lead this spiritually and mentally "messed-up" pastor's son to the Saviour. This *same* young man was the one who later in life penned the words of that great hymn…

Years I spent in vanity and pride,
Caring not my Lord was crucified,
Knowing not it was for me He died
Mercy there was great, and grace was free,
Pardon there was multiplied to me,
There my burdened soul found liberty,
At Calvary.

What happened to William Newell and thousands of others just like him? They got saved! The powerful Word of God *changed their **lives***, and they became *unshackled* of sin. By the way, do you know what happened to William R. Newell? Besides writing the beloved hymn "At Calvary" among others, he pastored a church in Chicago until 1895 when Moody invited him to become the assistant superintendent of Moody Bible Institute under R. A. Torrey, the man who originally led him to Christ. In this position Newell often demonstrated his extraordinary gift of Bible exposition. Great crowds flocked to hear the citywide Bible classes he held all over the world.

One of the proofs why God's Word is definitely inspired is because of its certain power to completely change and transform lives! Its changing of lives makes you believe the fact that the Bible *has* to be inspired by an awesome God!

CONCLUSION

We've taken a brief look at proofs of why God's Word is truly God's Word. First of all, the Bible claims it. Second, history and time reveal it. Third, fulfilled prophecies confirm it. Fourth, science agrees with it. And lastly, its changing of lives makes you believe it! These five proofs are enough to show that the Bible is God-breathed. There is no other religious book that man can offer to match the Bible. There is nothing, never has been, and never will be anything that will be able to compare to the Bible. The Bible has been proven to be *correct* and ***true*** by science, history, time, and people's lives. These five proofs have been clearly and accurately presented. We can **believe**—not assume—that this Book, the Bible, has absolutely, without a shadow of a doubt, been inspired by an Almighty God…Jehovah God.

Yes, atheists, liberals, and others will still stubbornly not yield from their unbelief. However, when you honestly look at the factual truth, there is too much evidence to *favor* the inspiration of the Bible than any supposed evidence *against* it.

CHAPTER III

THE PRESERVATION
OF THE BIBLE

Throughout the ages, God has preserved His inspired holy Word so that we as His children could have a copy of it today. God wanted for us to know the truth so that we would not be susceptible to error and falsehood. God wanted us to have His Word. It is fascinating to examine *how* He miraculously preserved it. There are two elementary principles that we must remember when we deal with the preservation of the holy Word of God.

BECAUSE OF WHAT GOD SAID

Though there are always people out there who want to destroy the precious pureness of the Bible's infallible inspiration, throughout time God has always preserved His Word.

The Everlasting God **promised** that His Word would remain indestructible. The Bible has been preserved for us today simply because God *said* so. He says in Isaiah 40:8 says, "The word of our God **shall** *stand for ever."* Notice that God said "shall." Not maybe, not might be, not possibly; but *shall* or *will* stand forever! *We still have the Bible today.*

Isaiah 55:11 says, "My word...**shall** *not return void."* That means that God's Word is not going to be an idle Book, but it is going to be affecting the lives of others.

Isaiah 59:21 says, "My words...***shall*** *not depart out of thy mouth...*" This gives us the idea that His words will always be there and will always be preserved.

Jesus Christ declares in Matthew 5:18, "One jot or one tittle ***shall in no wise*** pass from the law." In other words, not one small letter or one small *part* of a letter will **ever** vanish from the preserved Bible. Christ tells us in Matthew 24:35, "My words ***shall not*** pass away." Again He says in Luke 16:17, "And it is easier for heaven and earth to pass, *than one tittle of the law* ***to fail.***" It is easier for the *universe* to be *no more*, than for the dot over the "i" to fail in being preserved by God for us! Christ declared that the Bible is indestructible, imperishable, permanent, everlasting, and is going to remain perpetually unharmed. It has never failed; it has never vanished; it has never faded away. It always has been; it still is; and it always will be. Thank God that He has preserved His Word!

Benjamin Warfield once said, "If we compare the present state of the New Testament text with that of *any other* ancient writing, we must...declare it to be marvelously correct. Such has been the care with which the New Testament has been copied—a care which has doubtless grown out of true reverence for its holy words—*such has been* ***the providence of God*** *in preserving for His Church in each and every age a completely* ***exact*** *text of the Scriptures.*" God has preserved His Word for us because He *said* so.

Because of What God's Men Have Done

God's men took the preservation and the copying of the Bible *seriously* (which is the correct way to approach the Word of God). They, with a complete reverence and awe toward it, kept God's Word preserved—word for word from accepted, inspired, ancient manuscripts.

The early Jews took *much* care in copying the Old Testament. Their sacred approach to Scripture was adopted by Christians, and they, too, followed similar careful instructions when they copied both the Old and the New Testaments.

Listen to the Talmud's minute guidelines that the Jewish scribes went by as they seriously copied God's inspired Holy Old Testament of Scripture.

*A synagogue roll must be written on the skins of clean animals.... These must be fastened together with strings taken from clean animals. Every skin must contain a certain number of columns, equal throughout the entire codex [manuscript]. The length of each column must not extend over less than forty eight, or more than sixty lines; and the breadth must consist of thirty letters. The whole copy must be first lined; and if three words be written in it without a line, it is worthless. The ink should be black, neither red, green, nor any other colour, and be prepared according to a definite receipt [recipe]. An authentic copy must be the exemplar, from which the transcriber ought **not** in the least to deviate. No word or letter, not even a yod, must be written from memory, the scribe not having looked at the codex before him.... Between every consonant the space of a hair or thread must intervene; between every word the breadth of a narrow consonant; between every new parshiah, or section, the breadth of nine consonants; between every book, three lines.... Besides this, the copyist must sit in full Jewish dress, wash his whole body, not begin to write the name of God with a pen newly dipped in ink, and should a king address him while writing that name he **must** take no notice of him.... The rolls in which these regulations are not observed are condemned to be buried in the ground or burned....*

As you can see from this Talmud excerpt, these faithful men who preserved God's Word treated it as sacred and holy when they copied it. *So ought we.* That same Book that these copyists took so much time over is *the same Bible that we have today.* It's unfortunate, but the same Bible that these copyists spent so much time over with absolute reverence and carefulness hundreds of years ago, is the same Book that we now toss aside on our dressers half the time, never taking the time to genuinely read it.

Do you realize what they went through in order *for us* to have an accurately *preserved* copy of the Word of God? English translators (such as William Tyndale and John Wycliffe) gave their lives to carefully copy the Word of God without any incorrect words or grammatical errors in order to produce an *accurately preserved* English Bible. There is no other book that copyists have ever sacrificed so much time, lives, and personal plans for.

There has not been *one single book that mankind has so revered and more carefully treated and preserved throughout all of history than **the inspired Word of God** itself!* Copyists would count *each* sentence, *each* word, and *each* letter to make sure that not even the slightest error was present or any wrongfully written letter of a word was found. If an error was found upon a page, they would immediately *tear* it up and rewrite it.

As they copied, before they penned *each* word (and *never* writing one word from memory), they would say it out loud and *then* write it onto the parchment.

Before they wrote the name of God, they would wipe their pens and say His name in prayer. *Every time* when they came to God's most precious and holy name—JEHOVAH—they would wash their whole bodies as if they were an unclean vessel, unworthy to write that Supreme name of God.

After all of the copying was completed, it was then compared with the accepted ancient manuscript from which it was copied. If there was *one wrong letter or inaccuracy,* the **entire** copy was **rejected!**

How serious and sacred these copyists treated the inspired Word of **God**. You may think that they might have gone "overboard" with it, but I for one am so *thankful* that they were passionately zealous for total accuracy so that you and I could possess an unadulterated, error-free, totally *preserved*, God inspired, copy of the Holy Scriptures.

We need to realize the seriousness of the preservation of the Bible. It was not some easy task, but men took their time and repenned the same words from an ancient manuscript to another fresh new one over and over again.

We need to thank God for doing what He did for us. We ought to thank God that He preserved His Word, so that we might have His whole Word *today*.

Through this chapter, we have seen it's quite evident that the Bible has truly been preserved because of what God said and because of what God's men have *willingly* done.

CHAPTER IV

ABOUT THE APOCRYPHA

Some of you may have never heard of the Apocrypha. The *Apocrypha* is a collection of books written mainly during the 400-year period of silence between the Old and New Testaments. One of the common places you will find the Apocrypha is in the Catholic Bible. They and others still observe it as apart of the Bible.

There are many reasons why we do not accept this collection of books as part of the inspired, preserved Word of God.

- The Apocrypha does not *claim* to be inspired of God.

- The Apocrypha was not accepted as the Inspired Word of God by the Jewish Christians.

- Jesus Christ never *once* mentioned them in *any* of His sermons nor did He sanction them.

- For the first 400 years of the Christian church, it was not accepted to be the Word of God until the Catholic church endorsed it.

- The Apocrypha is loaded with historical and chronological errors. For instance, Tobit claims to have been alive as a youth when Jeroboam and the Ten

Northern Tribes of Israel revolted in 931 B.C. against King Rehoboam. Then he said that he was *also* alive when Assyria conquered Israel in 722 B.C. These two events were separated by over 200 years and yet the total lifespan of Tobit was 158 years (Tobit 1:3-5; 14:11)! The book of Judith mistakenly identifies Nebuchadnezzar as king of the Assyrians (Judith 1:1,7) when in fact he was the king of Babylon (2 Kings 24:1).

•   The Apocrypha contradicts doctrinally with the Bible.

We *know* that the Bible does not and never will contradict itself. So either the Apocrypha is right and the Bible is wrong, or the Apocrypha is wrong and the Bible is right. Let's take a look at six doctrinal errors found in the Apocrypha that the inspired Word of God would *never* ordain.

Salvation by Good Works

Tobit 12:9 says, "For **alms** doth deliver from death, and shall purge away all sin. Those that exercise **alms and righteousness** shall be filled with life." Sirach 3:30 says, "Water will quench a flaming fire; and alms maketh an atonement for sin." However, the Bible tells us in I John 1:7 that "**the blood of Jesus** Christ his Son cleanseth us from all sin." No, it is not by giving money to the poor or putting money into the church offering plate but by the shed blood of Jesus Christ all our sins shall be washed away.

Sirach 3:3 says, "Whoso **honoureth his father** maketh an *atonement for his sins.*" Nowhere in the Bible does it teach that you can go to Heaven if you obeyed your parents enough when you were a child. Rather, it teaches *"Children, obey your parents in the Lord: for this is right. Honour thy father and mother; (which is the first commandment with promise;) That it may be well with thee, and thou mayest live long on the earth"* (Ephesians 6:1-3). God says in the Ten Commandments, *"Honour thy father and thy mother: that thy days may be long upon the land which the LORD thy God giveth thee"* (Exodus 20:12). God wants us to obey and honour (immediate obedience with loving respect) our parents not to get saved but *"that it may be well with thee, and thou mayest live long on the earth"* (Ephesians 6:3). We obey so that we might have a long, prosperous, and good life.

There is no work, deed, or action we can do to get saved on our own; salvation is totally by the grace of God through the blood of Christ. Ephesians 2:8-9 says, "For by grace are ye saved through faith; and that not of yourselves: it is the gift of God: ***Not of works,*** lest any man should boast." It's nothing we can do; it's totally through Christ.

Casting Out demons by Magic

This "practice" is directly taught in Tobit 6-8. Tobit 6:6-7 says, *"Then the young man said to the angel, Brother Azarias, to what use is the heart and the liver and the gal of the fish? And he said unto him, Touching the heart and the liver, if a devil or an evil spirit trouble any, we must make a smoke thereof before the man or the woman, and the party shall be no more vexed."*

This is witchcraft "magic." Magic has never been used in the Bible to cast out devils – only Divine *miracles* or the mighty hand of God can accomplish that. In his 1828 Dictionary, Noah Webster defines *magic* as "the art or science of putting into action the power of spirits; or the science of producing wonderful effects by the aid of superhuman beings, or of departed spirits; sorcery; enchantment." Further down in the definition he mentions the various types of magic. "Superstitious or geotic magic" is the one referred to in the Apocrypha. He explains that it "consists in the invocation of devils or demons, and supposes some tacit or express agreement between them and human beings."

God tells us specifically in Deuteronomy 18:10-12: "There shall not be found among you any one that maketh his son or his daughter to pass through the fire, or that useth divination, or an observer of times, or an enchanter, or a witch, or a charmer, or a consulter with familiar spirits, or a wizard, or a necromancer. For *all* that do *these things* are an **abomination** unto the LORD: and because of these abominations the LORD thy God doth drive them out from before thee." God hates magic and is against *anybody* who is associated with it. They are an *abomination* unto Him.

This is a very serious thing with God. It is something not to mess around with. He gives us a punishment for it in Leviticus 20:27, "A man also or woman that hath a familiar spirit, or that is a wizard, *shall* **surely** be put to death." The punishment is severe. *It is death*, the same for the murderer (see Genesis 9:8).

The Bible even **commands** us in Leviticus 19:31, "Regard *not* them that have familiar spirits, **neither seek after wizards**, to be **defiled** by them: I am the LORD your God." Young person, this *would* include Harry Potter. God **commands** us to not associate with these types of people. *"Regard them **not**; neither seek after them."* Trust Him; God has your best interests in mind. He knows what will be helpful for you and what will be harmful. If He tells us to pay no attention to it and to not "seek" after it, don't you think that's the best thing you could ever do? Some say, "Well, Harry Potter is not that bad." Well, the original intention of the series was for witchcraft. The woman who wrote the Harry Potter series openly admitted on the news in Europe that she is a **witch** and that *she wants to introduce* **witchcraft** *to young people through her books.* I believe God is saying, *"Regard him not; neither seek after him."* God gave us these commands to keep ourselves from being *defiled*. God wants us to keep ourselves clean and pure. When you delve into it, you only open yourselves up for attacks from the Demonic Forces of Evil.

THE USE OF MAGIC IN HEALING

Tobit 11:11-13 relates, "And took hold of his father: and he strake of the gall on his fathers' eyes, saying, Be of good hope, my father. And when his eyes began to smart, he rubbed them; And the whiteness pilled away from the corners of his eyes: and when he saw his son, he fell upon his neck." We saw moments ago that God is against witchcraft. Does God contradict Himself? *No.* Obviously He would not say one thing, then turn around and teach something else.

There is a correct way to heal – not by magic, but by a miracle. Jesus Christ is the Great Physician – the Ultimate M.D. He is still in the healing business; He is very busy and good at His profession.

We must pray to Him and ask Him to help our friends or family in need of healing. If we pray in absolute faith and if it is His Will, Jesus will hear us and perform His healing power. We have all seen this come about time and time again. We don't need to perform some type of magical ritual like the heathen, but pray with patience and passion in faith.

SUICIDE

Suicide is taught through the example of a man named Nicanor in II Maccabees 14:41-46. The account is rather unpleasant so I've decided not to put the passage here for us to read.

However, is suicide wrong? And if so, why?

The Bible says in Exodus 20:13 and Deuteronomy 5:17, "Thou shalt not kill." God is telling us *not* to murder. What is suicide? It is the killing or *murdering* of our own self. God distinctly tells us **NO. It's wrong. "Thou shalt not!"**

The Bible also says in I Corinthians 6:19-20, "*What?* know ye not that your body is the *temple of the **Holy Ghost*** which is in you, which ye have of God, and *ye are not your own?* For ye are bought with a price: therefore glorify God in your body, and in your spirit, ***which are God's.***" God is saying here, "What? Don't you know that your body is not yours, but it is mine? Hey, I bought you… I bought you with a price, and that price was my only begotten Son to save your soul." Our bodies belong to God. So what right do we really have to take our own life when it is God's? We should take care of our bodies as if we're taking care of something very special and important that belongs to Him – for after all, it does!

THE INTERCESSION OF ANGELS

In Tobit 12:15, the Apocrypha says, "I am Raphael, one of the seven holy angels, *which present the prayers of the saints,* and which go in and out before the glory of the Holy One."

Many millions of people are enslaved to the belief that angels, saints, or Virgin Mary can intercede for them before God. In the Catholic religion, people go to confession booths and privately confess their sins to a priest. Yet, the Bible teaches something different. The Word of God reveals that only the Holy Spirit and Jesus Christ intercede for us, and *not* an angel called Raphael or any other being.

The Bible teaches that one of the "jobs" of the *Holy Spirit of God* is to make intercession for us. Romans 8:26-27 says, *"Likewise the Spirit also helpeth our infirmities: for we know not what we should pray for as we ought: but* **the Spirit itself maketh intercession for us with groanings which cannot be uttered***. And he that searcheth the hearts knoweth what is the mind of the Spirit, because he maketh intercession for the saints according to the will of God."*

On several occasions the Bible teaches us that Jesus *also* intercedes for us on our behalf. He intercedes for us before God the Father in the acts of salvation and forgiveness.

Jesus made intercession for us on the cross of Calvary. Isaiah 53:12 tells us that He *"was numbered with the transgressors; and he bare the sin of many, and* **made intercession for the transgressors***."* Romans 8:34 says, *"Who is he that condemneth? It is Christ that died, yea rather, that is risen again, who is even at the right hand of God, who also maketh intercession **for us**."* Hebrews 7:25 says, *"Wherefore he is able also to save them to the uttermost that come unto God by him,* **seeing he ever liveth to make intercession for them***."* Jesus Christ was the only Person able to bring God and man together, and He made a way by coming down to this earth, dying on an old rugged Cross, and *shedding His precious blood.*

When we ask Jesus to save us, our sins will be covered by His blood and washed away. The shed blood of Christ will make us look complete and righteous in the sight of the Heavenly Father as He down upon us from Heaven. Jesus intercedes for us *in the act of salvation.*

Jesus continues to make intercession once we are saved. We will never be perfect, but we should strive to be as much as possible. There will be many times in our lives and even moments every day that we will do wrong and sin against God. As a child of God we need to ask for forgiveness for our sin (**not** get saved again) to clear our relationship with the Lord so that we might continue to walk in His blessings. When we do this, Christ *intercedes* for us and wipes away our sin with His blood to make us complete again in the sight of God. Jesus intercedes for us *in the act of forgiveness.*

So we clearly see from the Bible that the Holy Spirit intercedes for our *supplications* (our prayers), and Jesus Christ intercedes for our *soul* in salvation and in forgiveness. There is no reference to an angel or some other person who intercedes to God for us!

Sinless Lives of Abraham, Isaac, and Jacob

This false teaching is mentioned in the book of Manasseh, which consists of his prayer to God. Manasseh says to God in a portion of his prayer, "Abraham, and Isaac, and Jacob…have not sinned against thee."

Though these three men were good, Godly men, they *all* were sinners. *"For all have **sinned**, and come short of the glory of God.* (Romans 3:23)*"* Is this true or not? Of course it is.

God hates sin. The Bible says in Proverbs 6:16-19, *"These six things **doth the LORD hate**: yea, seven are an abomination* [utterly detestable] *unto him: A proud look, a lying tongue, and hands that shed innocent blood, An heart that deviseth wicked imaginations, feet that be swift in running to mischief, A false witness that speaketh lies, and he that soweth discord among brethren."* God *hates* sin, but He does *not* hate the sinner. God will always love them no matter what sin they commit. Think of King David. David committed adultery with Bathsheba and murdered her husband Uriah to cover up their illegitimate child. Yet God still loved him, and David has always been known as a man after God's own heart. Abraham sinned, but God still loved him. Isaac sinned, but God still loved him, too. Jacob sinned, but God loved him as well.

It was recorded twice in Genesis (once in Genesis 12:10-20 and again in Genesis 20:1-18) that Abraham had *"a lying tongue."* God hates "a lying tongue" according to Proverbs 6. Twice he told authorities that Sarah, his own wife, was his sister.

Abraham also did not follow God's plan but listened to his wife instead. God had told Abraham that He would raise up a seed through Abraham and *his wife Sarah,* not Abraham and some other woman who wasn't his wife. But Sarah insisted that her husband have a relationship with her handmaiden to bear him a man child. It is a sin to do something contrary to the will of God and to commit adultery.

One other time, Abraham did not take God seriously and doubted Him. When God said that he and his wife would have a son, Abraham laughed and questioned in his heart, "Shall a child be born unto him that is an hundred years old? And shall Sarah that is ninety years old, bear?" He figured God might have been "kidding." God does not "joke" or "kid." Kidding is not telling the truth only in a joking manner, but it really still is sin. God does not lie. It is impossible for Him to not tell the truth. Abraham was not sinless as the Apocrypha teaches in the prayer of Manasseh. However, God still *loved* Abraham, and Abraham is known as the "Friend of God." What a privilege to have that title.

Isaac, the son of Abraham, also had *"a lying tongue."* In Genesis 26:6-16 he was telling everybody that his wife Rebekah was only his sister. Revelation 21:8 says that *"all **liars,** shall have* *their part in the lake which burneth with fire and brimstone."* He deserved Hell-fire like anyone else. Yet God loved him *anyway,* and Isaac was still God's friend and servant. Since he *had* done wrong, he *could not possibly be sinless* as the Apocrypha teaches.

Jacob, the grandson of Abraham and the son of Isaac, had *"an heart that deviseth wicked imaginations"* and *"a lying tongue."* In Genesis 27, Jacob disguised himself as his oldest brother Esau. Jacob was a smooth man while his brother Esau was very hairy. One way their almost-blind father Isaac could tell them apart was by feeling their arms and the back of their neck. In Genesis 27, Isaac felt like he was on the point of death and requested that his oldest son Esau go out and kill a deer and prepare his favorite stew. Isaac promised his son that after he ate, he would pass onto him the blessing of the firstborn. Rebekah overheard this in the other room and desired rather Jacob to receive this blessing. Therefore, she made goat's skin for Jacob to put on his hands and his neck. They prepared a similar dish to what Esau would be making. Then Jacob *dressed* in one of his brother's outfits so he could smell and feel like his brother, *deceived* his father when he appeared, and he *lied* to him that he *was* Esau. Jacob pulled it off. He wound up effectively deceiving his father and receiving the blessing.

God plainly says in Psalms 101:7, *"He that worketh deceit shall not dwell within my house: he that telleth lies shall not tarry in my sight."* Even though Jacob committed these two sins that God despises, in the next chapter (Genesis 28) Jacob is at Bethel, fleeing for his life. At Bethel, he saw and met Jehovah God Himself. As Jacob slept, in a vision he saw a ladder emerge that went up to heaven with angels descending and ascending on it; at the top of that celestial ladder was *God.* There God confirmed the Abrahamic covenant with Jacob—this deceiver and liar.

Jacob also committed the sin of bigamy (being married to two women at the same time). God originally made marriage for one man and one woman united as one flesh. *Not* one man with two or three women joined together to be one flesh. In Genesis 29 the Bible tells us about Jacob working seven years to be able to marry Rachel. At the end of these seven years, Jacob (the deceiver) was deceived, and the Bible says he found out in the morning it was Leah that he had married instead of Rachel. However, because of his deep love for Rachel, Jacob promised Laban another seven years of labor if he could marry his other daughter Rachel.

Jacob wound up marrying two women. Rachel he dearly loved and Leah he hated in his heart (see Genesis 29:31-32). This was *another* transgression. God commands men, "Husbands, *love* your wives." *Not* hate. *Not* put up with them. But **love** them. This is unconditional.

Yet throughout all the mistakes and sins that Jacob committed, God still dearly loved him. Yes, God hated his sins, but *He did not* hate him. Jacob became a very special person. Later in his life, God renamed Jacob "Israel," after whom the entire race of God's chosen people was named. They became known as Israelites…the descendants of Israel, Jacob the deceiver.

CONCLUSION

There are *weighty* reasons that prove to us why the Apocrypha can**not** be part of God's Word.

The Apocrypha is not very well known today, and I wonder if you have ever heard about it in detail before you read this chapter. But it's good to be aware of it, because some consider it part of the Word of God. Watch out for it. As you witness to people, help others realize that it is not inspired of God.

CHAPTER V

THE ORIGINS OF THE KING JAMES BIBLE

The history of the King James Bible is fascinating. It is very interesting how God brought His Word into the English language and into its final form of the King James Bible for us.

HISTORICAL BACKGROUND

In the heart of the Middle Ages, God began to stir among the Christians in England. Men of God realized that their people needed a copy of the Bible in their own language. One such man was John Wycliffe.

By the time Wycliffe, a chief scholar in his day, came on the scene, the Roman Catholic Church believed it was unnecessary, even dangerous for people to read the Word of God. Therefore, the church taught only the priests, and they in turn would tell the people what they needed to know about the things of God (though heavily perverted by the church's dogma). This greatly discouraged education. During the Middle Ages, only few were educated and most people could not read or write. The common man knew nothing spiritually anyway, because all of their Catholic services were conducted in Latin and not in English.

John Wycliffe observed this spiritual plight and saw the spiritual darkness of his fellow countrymen. How they were blinded from the true saving Gospel through worship to church idols of saints and Mary, by the "pagan" Roman Catholic mass ceremonies, by the cultic and cannibalistic teaching of transubstantiation, and by the sacrament works-type salvation. His spirit was stirred within him to help his fellow countrymen, to spread the truth, and to expose the falsehoods of the Catholic church. He and his followers (called "Lollards" by their enemies) spread Bible doctrines throughout all of England by distributing tracts *written in English* to the people. Those that could read, read them to others; and his series of tracts spread like wildfire throughout England. To counterattack this sudden wave of people turning from the errors of the Church to the truths of the Bible expounded upon by Wycliffe, the Church began bitterly persecuting Wycliffe and his followers. Yet, throughout it all, John Wycliffe stood strong and stated: *"I believe that in the end the truth will **conquer**."*

With all that he had done, Wycliffe realized that his people needed the Word of God in their own hands, *written in their own language.* Though his enemies (the Church and its crowd) severely opposed him, he prevailed through the power of God. In 1378, John Wycliffe completed translating the New Testament. A few years later, he was able to finish translating the whole Word of God *into English for the first time.*

Because he was unfamiliar with Hebrew and Greek (which was common among the scholars in that day), Wycliffe could not produce a Bible from the Hebrew Old Testament and the Greek New Testament texts. Therefore, he had to directly translate this first English Bible from the Latin Vulgate, a Bible translated from the Hebrew and Greek into Latin in A.D. 350 by a brilliant man named Jerome. Even though the Latin Vulgate contained unbiblical doctrine, error, mistranslations, and corruption heavily influenced by the Roman Catholic Church, it was all in God's plan. God used this to introduce a "preliminary" translation of the Scriptures into the English language.

In the end, the truth conquered. The victory had been won, and God was triumphant. Satan and his Church were defeated. For the first time, the Word of God was finally translated into the English language.

In the year 1516 (sixty years after the invention of the movable type printing press and one year before Martin Luther nailed the 95 Thesis to the church door and sparked the beginning of the Protestant Reformation), Desiderius Erasmus (claimed to be the most brilliant Bible scholar out of the Renaissance time period) produced an accurately compiled Greek New Testament of Scripture, based on the uncorrupted, accurately-preserved, perfectly copied Greek manuscripts handed down from generation to generation. This new Greek New Testament text, later called the *Textus Receptus*, freed Christendom from the Latin Vulgate and all of the Catholic doctrines and Biblical errors. Bible scholars no longer had to use the Latin Vulgate or look at individual Greek manuscripts, but could go to the *Textus Receptus*, the true compilation of the *accurately* preserved and copied New Testament Greek manuscripts combined into one accurate Greek New Testament. The *Textus Receptus* eliminated any fallible teachings inserted by man and left only the infallible truths written by the hand of God.

When William Tyndale was still a young man studying the Word of God and preparing to become a scholar, he was significantly influenced by this same Desiderius Erasmus during Erasmus's second visit to England from 1509 to 1514.

Starting at the age of 25, Tyndale eagerly began to translate portions of the New Testament from Erasmus's *Textus Receptus* into the English language. Yet when the Church found out what he was doing, they persecuted him and made him flee the country for his life.

Settling in Germany, Tyndale continued to translate. *Ten years later in 1526 William Tyndale finished his work.* He and his men began smuggling this new translation of the Bible into England one copy at a time. Now for the first time, the English-speaking people were able to hold a completely accurate, inspired, and preserved New Testament of the Word of God in their hands.

Tyndale began translating the Old Testament into the English language right away. By 1530 he had successfully translated the first five books of the Bible but could not complete his work, because his enemies discovered his location and began hunting him all over Europe.

Meanwhile, back in England, Tyndale's associate, Miles Coverdale, picked up where Tyndale left off and completed Tyndale's translation of the Old Testament for him. In 1535, this Bible (known as the Coverdale Bible) was the first completed English Bible ever to be printed on the moveable type printing press. This made the publication and mass distribution of the Bible much easier. Englishmen were able to get their hands on the Bible much more quickly.

While all of this was going on, unfortunately, Tyndale's enemies caught up with him back on the continent of Europe and handed him over to the Catholic authorities. They, in turn, pronounced him a heretic and condemned him to be executed. In 1536, Tyndale was publicly executed, being strangled, then his body thrown into the fire. As the choking collar slipped around his neck and was tightened, the last recorded statement he made before he died was, *"Lord, open the King of England's eyes!"*

God heard his prayer and answered it. A few years before Tyndale's death, Henry VIII, King of England, severed the ties between England and the Roman Catholic Church. Though the Church of England (in many aspects, the same as the Roman Catholic Church only having a different name) was in power, a few religious freedoms were granted. Henry VIII also decreed in 1539 for English Bibles to be printed and one to be given to every church in the country. Now *all* the people had access to the Word of God **translated into their own language** *by the work of William Tyndale himself.*

The Bible that was printed and set up in all of the churches across England was called the "Great" Bible because of its large size. The "Great" Bible was composed mainly of the translations by William Tyndale and Miles Coverdale. These Bibles were chained (to prevent *theft,* ironically) to podiums, allowing people to come freely to read or hear the Word of God. Many times, people thronged around the pulpit in hushed excitement focused on every word read aloud in their own language.

Though William Tyndale was slaughtered, his life's vision had been accomplished. *It became a reality.* His Bibles were being read all over the country by the wealthy and the poor in their own language.

For a number of years, the English people enjoyed their few religious freedoms...until Mary Tudor, the first daughter of Henry VIII became queen of England. She reigned with terror from 1553 to 1558. Being staunchly Roman Catholic, she violently demanded that the people forsake their Bibles, recant their Bible beliefs, and revert once again to Roman Catholicism. Those who refused to recant were imprisoned in England's filthy, dingy, disease-ravaged dungeons; they were horrendously tortured until they either recanted or were put to death. Though some fled the country—mainly going to Geneva, Switzerland—many of the English people stood undauntedly and endured severe persecution.

Three hundred men, women, and children were burnt at the stake for their beliefs. John Rogers, the man of God that produced the Matthew's Bible, was one of these martyrs. "Bloody" Mary's persecution defeated its purpose. It wound up only strengthening the English people's faith. The more people were martyred, the more people took a stand for the Word of God and what was right.

In November of 1558, the next monarch took over the throne. She was the other daughter of Henry VIII and half sister to "Bloody" Mary, Queen Elizabeth I. Since she was a Protestant, religious persecution immediately ceased when she became queen, and many of the English Bible-believing Christians were welcomed back as they returned to England from Geneva and other places in continental Europe. Queen Elizabeth I became well loved by her people and was known as "Good Queen Bess."

The English Christians returning from Geneva, Switzerland, brought back with them a new and more accurate English translation of the Word of God into the English language. Many of England's scholars worked together in Geneva during their exile to produce this translation. Because of where (location) it came from, it became known as the "Geneva Bible" and caught on like wildfire all across England after it was produced and printed in 1560. It became the most popularly-used English Bible around, and was the same Bible used by William Shakespeare, John Milton, John Bunyan, and the Separatist Pilgrims who came over on the *Mayflower* to their new establishment in Massachusetts, America.

It is very significant to note that the Geneva Bible was the first English Bible to have its entire Old Testament directly translated from Hebrew. This had never been done before. (Notice that each translation of the Bible produced a more purified and finalized "version" of the Word of God in our English language.)

For roughly fifty years, the Geneva Bible was the most widely used Word of God in England. In the year 1603, Queen Elizabeth I died without an heir to sit on the throne. The royal authorities in the English government decided to pass the scepter onto King James VI of Scotland.

King James was born in 1567 and was crowned King of Scotland at the age of only thirteen months. When he accepted the English crown, he united England and Scotland together and reigned as King James I.

King James was one of the first kings in Europe to encourage the propagation of the Bible in the language of the people. He wanted the Word of God to be in the hands, the hearts, and the homes of his subjects, not chained to the pulpits or read only by scholars and theologians.

He continued to support the printing of the Geneva Bible in England, though he didn't like some of the marginal notes in it because of its strong opinions against the throne and the Church of England.

His desire was the same as Queen Elizabeth I – an English Bible for the English Christians and churches produced on *English soil*.

"In 1604 John Rainolds approached the king with the idea of a new translation of the Bible to be produced in England. King James welcomed the suggestion, and commissioned fifty-four of the greatest scholars the world has ever known to produce this new Bible. 'All principal learned men of the kingdom' were also extended an invitation to participate in this greatest of endeavors."[1]

"Of the fifty-four men selected, four were college presidents, six were bishops, five were University deans, thirty were Ph.D.s, thirty-nine had Master of Arts degrees, forty-one were University professors, thirteen were highly skilled Hebrew scholars, ten were highly skilled Greek scholars, and three were eastern linguists who were as fluent in Arabic as in English.

"All fifty-four men believed in the verbal plenary inspiration of the Scriptures and the deity of Christ. All fifty-four were men of prayer."[2]

"In 1607 the work began. Forty-seven men remained of the fifty-four originally selected. Some had died. Some had resigned due to ill health or other unforeseen circumstances."[3]

"The forty-seven men on the translation committee were divided into six companies consisting of six to eight men each, which met in three locations across England, in Cambridge, Oxford, and Westminster Abbey. The entire text of the Bible was divided into six portions and each of the six committees received a portion to translate. Each man in each committee personally translated the entire portion of Scripture his committee had been assigned, then the whole committee met together and reviewed one another's work. Until they came to one hundred percent unanimous consensus that what they had produced was an accurate, faithful, correct translation of the Word of God into the English language, the work never went beyond that committee."[4]

The six translation boards that were commissioned by King James went back to the original Hebrew and Greek languages to make an accurate and correct word-for-word *finalized* translation of the Word of God into the English language. (As we discuss the textual background of where we got the King James Bible in the next section, we will explain *which* Hebrew and Greek texts these men of God used to accurately produce a finalized English Bible).

"Each portion of the Bible from each committee passed through all six committees' hands for review. All six committees had to agree by one hundred percent unanimous consent that the translation was accurate, faithful, and correct before each section of the Bible left each committee.

"Then a **seventh** and final review committee met in 1610 and for one year perused the finished product. They, too, came to a one hundred percent unanimous vote that what they had produced was 'one more exact translation of the holy Scriptures in the English tongue.' 'The words of the Lord are pure words... purified **seven** times.'"[5]

"The first printing was completed in 1611, exactly **seven** years from the initiation of the project."[6]

Thousands of copies of the Authorized Version were printed in 1611. One Bible was to be placed in each of the pulpits of the twenty thousand churches in England. These were large, ornate, beautiful Bibles, known as 'pulpit Bibles.' Beginning the following year, in 1612, smaller editions were also produced, encouraging individuals to have their own personal copy of the Word of God for study and for following the Scripture reading in church.

"It is remarkable that forty-seven of the greatest scholars ever assembled for one undertaking, utilizing a total of seven years' preparation and translation work, could improve on less than ten percent of the work of one man done more than eighty years earlier. The King James Bible translators retained more than ninety percent of the very words translated by William Tyndale in their finished product. The New Testament of the King James Version is almost word-for-word William Tyndale's translation. This is not only a tribute to Tyndale and the way God so greatly used him in giving the English speaking world a Bible of their own, it is also a tribute to the forty-seven translators of the Authorized Version, who, unlike the modern Bible producers, left well enough alone. Nine times out of ten they looked at Tyndale's Bible, then compared it with the plethora of manuscripts, versions and translations that lay before them, and concluded, 'Leave it alone. Tyndale got it right.' Their wise discernment in this matter was no doubt derived from another proverb with which we are so familiar – 'If it ain't broke, don't fix it!'"[7]

When the Bible was translated into the English language each version that was produced became closer and closer to that which was originally written by verbal plenary inspiration in the Hebrew Old Testament and the Greek New Testament.

The first translation was John Wycliffe's Bible translated from the Latin Vulgate in 1378, and the final was the 1611 King James Bible, translated accurately from the original Hebrew and Greek.

Now for four hundred years, the King James Bible has virtually remained the same. The only "changes" were not mistranslation changes. "Every change made to the King James Bible [since the very first printing in 1611] was an attempt to standardize spelling, correct punctuation, or correct a printer's error, and was not an attempt to retranslate a mistranslation, and was certainly not a departure from the *Textus Receptus* in favor of a Minority Text rendering. The text of the King James Bible is virtually and essentially unchanged from the first printing in 1611 to this very day. It is the same Book!"[8]

My friend, the King James Bible printed in England reads the same as the one printed in the United States and around the world. The King James Bible printed in 1611 reads the same as the King James Bible printed today!

TEXTUAL BACKGROUND

As we delve into the textual background of the King James Bible, we are going to separate the translations of the Old and New Testaments in our studies. Taking them one at a time will allow us to understand more easily.

Once you see the origins of the KJV textually, you will be firmly established *beyond a shadow of a doubt* in believing that the King James Bible is the *only* inspired, preserved Word of God for the English-speaking people.

THE OLD TESTAMENT

The Old Testament was primarily written in the Hebrew language. For thousands of years, Christians undoubtedly and unwaveringly held to the Masoretic Text—the traditional, handed down, Hebrew Old Testament—as the inspired, preserved Old

Testament of Scripture. Then in the early 1900's, a certain liberal German theologian and rationalist named Rudolph Kittel compiled a new Hebrew text different from the accepted Masoretic Text of the Old Testament. He named his new Hebrew text the *Biblia Hebraica.* The *Biblia Hebraica* originated from Hebrew manuscripts that had been rejected long ago for their significant error.

Rudolph Kittel was an agent for the Devil, believing in liberal, radical, unbiblical theology. Rudolph Kittel denied many key doctrines of Scripture and Fundamentals of the Faith. He did not believe in the inspiration and preservation of God's Word. He did not believe in Christ's virgin birth, Christ's deity, His miracles, or His glorious resurrection. Henry M. Morris, the founder of the Institute for Creation Research, claims that Kittel was a stanch evolutionist. Yet, many Christians slowly started to accept this liberal's new Hebrew text of the Old Testament, when in actuality—*he didn't even believe in it, denying key Scriptural doctrine.* I've got a big problem with that. Don't you? How can we trust someone to correctly handle the Bible when he does not even believe in Biblical inspiration [being God-breathed] and preservation? How can we trust someone like that when, in essence, he believes the Bible is just another "book"?

I don't trust him one bit. Why should we accept the *Biblia Hebraica* by German liberal, evolutionist, and rationalist Rudolph Kittel as the inspired Old Testament of the Bible if the Masoretic Text was good for our spiritual ancestors. If it was good enough for them (and we know that God doesn't change) *then it's still good enough for us!* Why do we have to have a new text of the Hebrew Old Testament when it was good enough for D. L. Moody, Charles Haddon Spurgeon, Sam Jones, and other great fundamental preachers back in the 1800s? When it was good enough for our Founding Fathers? When it was good enough for the Pilgrims?

Rudolph Kittel's own son, Gerhard Kittel, worked for the Third Reich and influenced many Germans to join in Hitler's slaughtering of the Jews—the Holocaust. As a result, after the WWII, Gerhard was tried and convicted for his horrible crimes against humanity. I wonder if the nut didn't fall very far from the tree. *Christians, scholars, and translators of today have accepted*

Gerhard Kittel's father's Hebrew Old Testament text, the Biblia Hebraica, as the inspired, preserved Old Testament of Scripture!

The King James Bible's Old Testament came directly from the Masoretic Text. All of the new, modern English translations of Scripture get their Old Testament translation mainly from the *Biblia Hebraica* compiled by Rudolph Kittel. In other words, the King James Bible contains the Old Testament that for thousands of years our spiritual ancestors accepted as God's inspired Word, but all the modern English versions contain an Old Testament originating from a perverted text by a theological and political liberal. This is a very strong statement, but it is very true.

THE NEW TESTAMENT

In the beginning of the New Testament times, the original epistles were penned by the writers through the Holy Spirit. From these original manuscripts came identical copies for other people or churches. Over time, there developed *three* groups or "families" of copies from these original epistles of the New Testament. They were the Traditional Text family, the Alexandrian Text family, and the Western Text family.

The Traditional Text family of the New Testament is the accurate copies of the *original* epistles. Through this family, God preserved His inspired Word. The *Textus Receptus*, complied by Desideruis Erasmus, was a compilation of the majority-accurate Traditional Text copies of the New Testament **into one accurate Greek New Testament**. From this compilation of the accurate Greek came the English New Testament for our King James Bible.

The Alexandrian Text family came out of a liberal Christian school in Alexandria, Egypt. These texts had actually *cut out* some passages of Scripture, making it shorter than the Traditional Text copies. The Alexandrian Text family also contained a lot of heresy, especially attacking the deity of Jesus Christ. From the Alexandrian text family came two main manuscripts the many recent translators refer to: the Sinaiticus and the Vaticanus.

These two manuscripts were unused for years. It is not difficult to see why – they were loaded with contradictions and mistakes. The Sinaiticus and the Vaticanus manuscripts contradicted each other in over **3,000** places in the Gospels alone. *They didn't even agree with each other.* Who would want to use something that's not correct? If these manuscripts were the inspired Word of God, they wouldn't have **once** contradicted each other – but would have been in absolute harmony. God's true inspired, correctly preserved Word remains without flaws and errors.

These two manuscripts, after they were "rediscovered," were used in 1881 by two men named Westcott and Hort to form a new type of "Textus Reptus" of the New Testament for "scholars" and Christians to use.

From the Westcott and Hort eclectic text of Scripture **came all the modern English translations of the New Testament.** From this majorly corrupt Westcott and Hort text came the American Standard Version, Moffat's Translation, the Revised Standard Version, Philip's New Testament, the New American Standard Version, the New English Bible, the New King James Version, the Living Bible, the Today's English Version, the Good News for Modern Man Version, the New International Version, and many other English versions of the Bible.

"Please read and re-read this next paragraph. Please allow this truth to sink in. The King James Bible was the last major English translation of the Scriptures to be based solely on the *Textus Receptus*—the Received Text, the traditional, time-honored, faithful, pure text of the Word of God, the text for which William Tyndale, Myles Coverdale, John Rogers, and so many other Christians have been persecuted and slain. There has not been one popular English translation of the Bible produced after the King James that came from the true Bible text – not one! God in His providence has seen to it that the King James Bible is His Book for the English-speaking world. Every modern English Bible comes from the perverted, corrupted text fabricated by Wescott and Hort, or at least borrows heavily from it. This cannot be overemphasized. You need to understand this

truth. **Any Bible produced since 1885 is not a Bible at all, but an erroneous departure from the Word of God. Do not settle for the devil's counterfeit!"**[9]

NOW…who exactly were these guys Westcott and Hort? Once they were dead it was discovered, to the shock of the Christian world, that *both of these men were dedicated* **spiritualists** *and* **Satanists** *involved heavily in the occult and necromancy.* So, let me get this straight—all the modern versions of the English Bibles get their New Testament translations from a contradicting, error-filled text compiled by two Satanists? Do you *think* we can trust such men to give us an accurate word-for-word New Testament Greek text? *Absolutely not.* Therefore, let's not use their Bibles.

The third family of texts from the original epistles is *the Western Text family.* From the Western Text family came the Latin Vulgate and the Roman Catholic Bible. The Western texts have also *added* things that the Traditional Text family and the Alexandrian texts of Scripture *did **not*** contain. In addition to this, these texts **delete** key doctrines of the Bible such as the blood atonement and Christ's ascension. Not only were the Alexandrian texts corrupt, but these Western texts were corrupt, as well.

I believe that the only logical conclusion that we can come to is that the King James Bible is clearly the *accurate,* inspired, preserved Word of God for the English-speaking people.

---

[1] Evangelist Bill Bradley, *Purified Seven Times: The Miracle of the English Bible* (Haines City, FL: Landmark Baptist Press, 2001), 107-108. (All quotations used by permission.)

[2] Ibid., 110.

[3] Ibid., 116.

[4] Ibid., 117-118.

[5] Ibid., 118.

[6] Ibid., 116.

[7] Ibid., 120-121.

[8] Ibid., 125.

[9] Ibid., 117.

ORIGINAL COPIES

Alexandrian Text Family

Traditional Text Family

Western Text Family

Sinaiticus & Vaticanus Manuscripts

Textus Receptus

All the Modern Corrupt Translations

INSPIRED KING JAMES VERSION

Latin Vulgate & Roman Catholic Bible

LINAGE OF THE NEW TESTAMENT TEXTS

CHAPTER VI

THE ISSUE OF THE
NEW KING JAMES VERSION

Many questions are raised about the New King James Version. And you might be wondering if the NKJV is really just a "new" King James Version only revised to today's grammatical standards. Well, let's find out if this is true.

The *New King James Version* was first published in 1979. According to the translators the NKJV was supposed to be just an updated form of the King James Bible and was supposed to be based on the *Textus Receptus*. These were their original intentions as stated in their brochure about the New King James Version:

• to use more reverent pronouns for God by removing "thee," "thou", and "ye"

• to update the punctuation and grammar

• to improve the understanding of verbs

• to capitalize pronouns for God

• to preserve the true meaning of words (this gives me the feeling that something is *wrong* with the King James

Version and translators needed to "rescue" it before it vanished away or failed to be God's Word anymore)

- to add quotation marks

- to protect theological terms

The Preface to the New King James Version (NKJV) reads, *"A special feature of the New King James Version is its **conformity** to the thought flow of the 1611 Bible…"* However, it turned out to become more than just that. The New King James Version is not actually what it seems to be. It is yet another corrupted version of the Word of God. There are three issues with the New King James Version that we must take note of: the issue of its substitutions, the issue of its sources, and the issue of its symbol.

THE ISSUE OF ITS SUBSTITUTIONS

The NKJV makes over 100,000 translation changes, which comes to *over eighty changes per page and about three changes per verse.* In addition to this, the NKJV removes 20,066 words from the original King James. A great number of these changes bring the NKJV in line with the NIV, the RSV, and others. Where changes are not made in the text, subtle footnotes often give credence to the Westcott and Hort Greek text that we talked about earlier.

The translators of the New King James Version even said in the notes section, *"It is clear that this revision required **MORE** than the dropping of 'eth' endings, removing 'thee's' and 'thou's', and updating obsolete words."* (*The New King James Version*, 1982 edition, page 1235).

In the NKJV, there are 23 omissions of "blood", 44 omissions of "repent," 50 omissions of "heaven," 51 omissions of "God," and 66 omissions of "Lord." The terms "devils," "damnation," "JEHOVAH," and "new testament" are omitted or replaced.

The NKJV demotes the Lord Jesus Christ. In John 1:3, the KJV says that all things were made "by" Jesus Christ, but in the NKJV, all things were just made "through" Him. The word "Servant" replaces "Son" in Acts 3:13 and 3:26. "Servant" replaces "child" in Acts 4:27 and 4:30. The word "Jesus" is omitted from Mark 2:15, Hebrews 4:8, and Acts 7:45. Another interesting thing is this. The New Age Movement and the occult are longing for one called the Maitreya. The Bible calls him the Anti-Christ. New Agers refer to him as the *"the Coming One." * **The NKJV refers to Christ as "the Coming One"** in Luke 7:19, 20 (also Matt 11:3). They translate John's instruction to his disciples to ask Jesus, *"Are You THE COMING ONE…"* "The Great Invocation," a "prayer" highly reverenced among New Agers and chanted to "invoke" the Maitreya, says, *"Let Light and Love and Power and Death, Fulfil the purpose of **the Coming One**."* That's kind of creepy!

The NKJV confuses people about salvation. In Hebrews 10:14 it replaces "are sanctified" with "are being sanctified", and it replaces "are saved" with "are being saved" in I Corinthians 1:18 and II Corinthians 2:15. The words "may believe" have been replaced with "may continue to believe" in I John 5:13. *This has opened the door for works salvation.* The NKJV gives us no command to "study" God's word in II Timothy 2:15.

The NKJV (and many other English versions) removes the word "hell" 23 times, and replaced it with "Hades" and "Sheol." This does not make things clearer but muddies it up, really. *Webster's New Collegiate Dictionary* defines "Hades" as "the underground abode of the dead in Greek **mythology**." In addition, Hades is not always a place of torment or terror as the true Hell of the Bible is. The Assyrian Hades is an abode of blessedness with silver skies called "Happy Fields." In the New Age Movement, Hades is an intermediate state of purification. "Hades" does not sound like the real "Hell" of the Bible that God made for the Satan and sin!

Many people seem to complain sometimes that the King James Bible is "difficult" to understand because it is written in a supposedly "old" style of English. The Preface to the NKJV states, "…thee, thou, and ye are replaced by the simple you,…**These**

pronouns are no longer part of our language." But "thee, thou and ye" were NO LONGER part of the language in 1611 either. (just read the introduction to the 1611 King James; there is no "thee", "thou", and "ye" in it.). The English of the King James Bible was not the English spoken in the 1600's when it was translated. The English used was very different from the English spoken in everyday speech in that time period. As a matter of fact, *it wasn't even a type of English ever spoken anywhere.* Page 2,648 of Webster's Third New International Dictionary says of "ye": "used from the earliest of times **to the late 13th century...**" And the 1611 King James was published 400 years later in the 17th century!

So why then were these "old words" used in the King James Bible? The reason is eye-opening. The Greek and Hebrew languages contain a different word for the second person singular and the second person plural pronouns; however, today we just use the word "you" for both singular and plural. But *because the translators of the 1611 King James Bible desired an accurate, word-for-word translation of the Hebrew and Greek text* – **they decided they *could not* just use the one-word "you" throughout.** Therefore, "thou", "thy", and "thine" were *singular*, but "ye" was *plural*. Isn't that clever and wonderful? Ads for the NKJV called it "the Accurate One," but in all reality that is far from true. The 1611 King James is more accurate by using "thee," "thou," and "ye" rather than just using a blanket "you."

The King James Bible English was its *own* style called "Biblical English." **This style of English was produced when the King James Bible was accurately and faithfully translated from the original Hebrew and Greek texts. The style of English of the King James Bible is that of the original Hebrew and New Testament Greek.**

Thomas Nelson Publishers made the claim in an ad for the NKJV (Moody Monthly, June 1982, back cover), **"NOTHING HAS BEEN CHANGED** except to make the original meaning clearer." I'm sorry, but sincerity can**not** improve on perfection. I'm afraid that instead of making "a good thing better" they only managed, for all of their trouble, to make a "perfect thing tainted."

THE ISSUE OF ITS SOURCES

What's more important is where the NKJV came from *textually*. What are its "roots" from the Hebrew and Greek. What Hebrew and Greek manuscripts was it translated from? Is it the same as the King James Bible?

We discussed how the Old Testament of the KJV was translated from the Masoretic Text. This faithful Rabbinic Old Testament was rejected by the NKJV committee in favor of a Vatican-published Hebrew text, the *Biblia Hebraica*, produced originally by *Rudolph Kittel*. Doesn't that name ring a bell?

The New Testament in the KJV was translated from the *Textus Receptus*. Remember, the *Textus Receptus*, complied by Desideruis Erasmus, was a compilation of the majority accurate Traditional Text copies of the New Testament **into one accurate Greek New Testament**. The NJKV New Testament was translated using Greek texts from primarily the Alexandrian and Western Text families, the Septuagint LXX, the Roman Catholic Latin Vulgate, the Majority Text, and others. Don't let the name "Majority Text" through you for a loop. You would think that if it had the name "Majority Text", then it *should* be a compilation of the **majority** of Greek New Testament manuscripts. But that is not so. The "Majority Text" is actually a hand-picked set of manuscripts grouped together by liberal scholar Hermann von Soden, who very much liked the Alexandrian Text family. Von Soden only used the manuscripts he liked to compile the Majority Text – less than **8%** of the over 5,000 Greek manuscripts were compared and used! This was NOT a true "majority" Text.

The fact is that in **most places where the NKJV disagrees with the King James Bible, it agrees with the Alexandrian text English Bibles,** whether Protestant like the NIV, NASV, RSV, ASV, and others, or Roman Catholic like the New American Bible.

My friend, the King James Bible is God's inspired, preserved Word of God for the English-speaking people. I believe that the NKJV is man's **most subtle perversion** of God's words. Please don't be deceived by it.

THE ISSUE OF ITS SYMBOL

So what is this "mysterious symbol" on the cover of the New King James Version?

Thomas Nelson Publishers (publishers of the NKJV) claim, on the inside cover, that it is "an ancient symbol for the Trinity." But the symbol has deeper history than this.

This symbol is called a *triquetra*. The triquetra was first found on ancient runestones in Northern Europe and on early Germanic coins and began with pagan religions. It bears a resemblance to the Valknut, a symbol associated with Odin, the chief god in Norse paganism.

The symbol was *later* adopted by "Christians" (mainly Catholics) as a symbol of the Trinity (Father, Son and Holy Spirit), since it conveniently incorporated three shapes locked together. However, God does not want us to do this. Acts 17:29 clearly says, "Forasmuch then as we are the offspring of God, *we ought **not** to think* that the Godhead is like unto gold, or silver, or stone, *graven by art and man's device*."

This symbol has always been used by pagans to symbolize a variety of concepts and mythological figures. Wiccans and New Agers use it to symbolize the Wiccan triple goddess, the interconnected parts of our existence (Mind, Body, and Soul), and many other concepts that seem to fit into this idea of a unity.

On page 150 in the book *Blood on the Doorposts,* former satanists Bill and Sharon Schnoebelen document that the triquetra is "a disguised interlocked trio of sixes. It also symbolizes the triple goddess of Wicca. Commonly used in Catholic liturgical iconography, **and has recently found its way into the logo of the New King James Bible**."

On pages 242-243, Dr. Cathy Burns writes in her book, *Masonic and Occult Symbols Illustrated*, concerning the symbol on the NKJV cover, "Marilyn Ferguson, a New Ager, used the symbol of the triquetra on her book *The Aquarian Conspiracy* (a handbook for the New Age Movement). **This is a variation for the number 666.** Other books and material have a similar design printed on them, such as books from David Spangler, the person who lauds Lucifer, and The Witch's Grimoire. As most people know, the number 666 is the number of the beast (see Revelation 13:18) and is evil, yet the occultists and New Agers love this number and consider it to be sacred. Many organizations, such as the World Future Society and the Trilateral Commission, incorporate this symbol into their logo. **I think it is quite interesting to see that this same symbol appears on the cover of the New King James Bible as well!**"

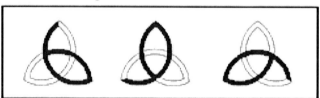

The Institute of
Transpersonal Psychology

The triqueta is used as the centerpiece for the logo for The Institute of Transpersonal Psychology (ITP). The ITP is a new age school following the Jungian Psychology [occultist Carl Jung]. One of their stated goals is ". . . to reach the recognition of divinity within."

The same symbol (with a circle) is displayed by the rock group Led Zeppelin. Members of Led Zeppelin are deeply involved in Satanism and the occult.

In recent years, the symbol has become well-known due to its use on the cover of the *Book of Shadows* used by the three sisters on the American TV show "Charmed." It represents the three sister witches working together as one. According to Jerry Johnston in his book *The Edge of Evil: The Rise of Satanism on North America* on page 269, The Book of Shadows is commonly used in witchcraft and Satanism. "**Book of Shadows** is also called a *grimoire*, this journal kept either by individual witches or Satanists or by a coven or group, records the activities of the group and the incantations used."

from the "Charmed" TV series

A necklace with the triquetra on it is used in the demonic film "Constantine," the story about a fallen angel who takes on human form to battle Satanic evil, giving its bearer what was described as being like a bulletproof vest, in the spiritual sense.

The Satanic band "Payable on Death" (P.O.D.) uses this symbol on most of their CD covers.

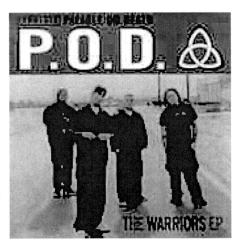

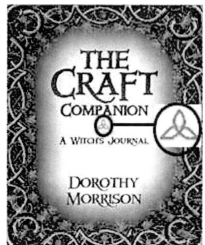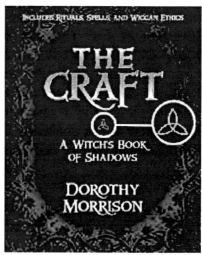

(Dorothy Morrison is a high priest of witchcraft.)

So we must ask ourselves a very obvious question, "Would God mark His Word with a symbol of the occult?" No. I believe this is a stamp of approval from Satan, authorizing use of this inaccurate version of the Bible.

THE PERVERSIONS OF ALL THE OTHER VERSIONS

In the beginning, Satan created and believed a perversion of the truth. He was kicked out of Heaven because of his five lies concerning himself. Commonly known as the "Five I Wills of Satan," they are mentioned in Isaiah 14:13-14, *"I will ascend into heaven, I will exalt my throne above the stars of God: I will sit also upon the mount of the congregation, in the sides of the north: I will ascend above the heights of the clouds; I will be like the most High."*

Satan is the Father of perversions—diluted and muddy forms of the truth. When he was tempting Jesus in the wilderness, Satan purposefully misquoted Scripture (recorded in Matthew 4:6) and twisted it *to mean what **he** wanted it to mean.*

Satan said, *"For it is written, He shall give his angels charge concerning thee: and in their hands they shall bear thee up, lest at any time thou dash thy foot against a stone."* In Matthew 4:6, Satan misquoted Psalms 91:11-12, taking out a phrase, then adding one. The Bible says in Psalms 91:11-12, *"For he shall give his angels charge over thee, to keep thee in all thy ways. They shall bear thee up in their hands, lest thy dash they foot against a stone."*

Satan was the first "new age translator" to have the Bible fit what he wanted it to say. Let's compare these two verses...

God's Version Versus Satan's Version

God's Version	Satan's Version
"For he shall give his angels charge *over* thee"	"For he shall give his angels charge *concerning* thee"
"To keep thee in all thy ways"	OMITTED by Satan
"They shall bear thee up in their hands"	"In their hands they shall bear thee up" [Reworded sentence by moving phrase "in their hands."]
"Lest thou dash thy foot against a stone."	"Lest at any time thou dash thy foot against a stone." [Added phrase "at any time."]

Clearly we can see that **Satan** is the father of the [per] versions of Scripture and the beginner of this anti-Bible rewriting process. A lifelong dream of his was fulfilled when the first perversion version of the Bible in the English language came out over a hundred years ago in 1885, the rest following soon after at a steadily increasing pace. There are hundreds of Bibles available for almost any kind of individual now-a-days. Here is only a partial list of some of the main Perversion Versions that most churches and Christians would use:

Partial List of the Perversion Versions

AMP—Amplified Version
ASV—American Standard Version
CEV—Contemporary English Version

KJ21—21st Century King James Version

LB—Living Bible

NAB—New American Bible

NASB—New American Standard Bible

NCV—New Century Version

NIV—New International Version

NIVI—New International Version Inclusive

NKJV—New King James Version

NLT—New Living Translation

NRSV—New Revised Standard Version

NWT—New World Translation

REB—Revised English Bible

RSV—Revised Standard Version

RV—Revised Version

TEV—Today's English Version (Good News For Modern Man)

In these perverted Bibles, many portions of Scripture have been "played" around with by the filthy hands of Satan and his men. Consider, for example, the New International Version. There are complete verses missing from the NIV such as Matthew 17:11, Matthew 17:21, Matthew 23:14, Mark 7:16, Mark 9:44, Mark 9:46, Mark 11:26, Mark 15:28, Luke 17:36, Luke 23:17, John 5:4, Acts 8:37, Acts 24:7, Acts 28:29, Romans 16:24, and I John 5:7. These listed verses are just a portion of the complete list. *(I strongly encourage you to take your King James Bible and read these verses to see the doctrine they are cutting out of the Word of God.)* Besides this, there are a number of portions of verses omitted, tens of thousands of words changed, and more than 200 times the names Jesus, Christ, and Lord deleted!

Let us take a handful of verses from the Bible and see how they have changed the wording.

PSALMS 12:6-7

The words of the LORD are pure words: as silver tried in a furnace of earth, purified seven times. **Thou shalt keep them**, *O LORD, thou* **shalt preserve** *them from this generation for ever.*

We can plainly see that the King James Bible is saying here that God is going to preserve **the words** of Scripture. Now I want you to notice how the new age versions (modern English [per] versions of Scripture) twist it around to fit what *they* want it to say. The new versions want you to believe that God is going to preserve His *people* rather than His *words*.

NIV — *you will keep us safe*

NASB — *Thou wilt preserve him*

NRSV — *You, O Lord, will protect us*

REB — *you are our protector*

LB — *you will forever preserve your own*

NAB — *You, O Lord, will keep us*

ISAIAH 7:14

Therefore the Lord himself shall give you a sign; Behold, **a virgin** *shall conceive, and bear a son, and shall call his name Immanuel.*

NRSV — *young woman*

REB — *young woman*

NIV — *young woman*

NWT — *maiden*

RSV — *young woman*

This is an attack on the Virgin Birth of Christ—one of the Fundamentals of the faith. There is a difference between a *young woman* or a *maiden* and a *virgin*. A virgin is a chaste, pure young lady who has never had a relationship with a man. However, a young woman or a maiden does not necessarily mean that. By using the word *virgin*, you are specific; but when you say *young woman* or *maiden*, you are vague. By using *young woman* or *maiden* you could mean a variety of things. About 85% of American young people lose their virginity by the age of 21. This slight rewording opens the doorway for non-Christians and other cults to have the Bible conform to what they believe. If Christ truly was not virgin born, then He would have been a sinner just like you and me. (The sin nature is passed through the bloodline of the *man*.) If Christ was not *virgin-born* then He would not have been able to die on the Cross and take away the sins of the world. We would be left without a Saviour and would still be on our way to Hell. We certainly would be of all men most miserable. So, do you see what changes when you alter just **one** *word of the Bible?*

ISAIAH 14:12

*How art thou fallen from heaven, O **Lucifer**, son of the morning! how art thou cut down to the ground, which didst weaken the nations!*

NIV — *morning star*

NASB — *star of the morning*

NRSV — *Day Star*

REB — *Bright morning star*

NWT — *you shining one*

NAB — *morning star*

Many modern translations change Satan's name, or they just remove it. The problem is that in Revelation 22:16 the Bible says *Jesus Christ* is the "Morning Star"—*not Satan.* Jesus Himself was speaking! "I Jesus have sent mine angel to testify unto you these things in the churches. I am the root and the offspring of David, and **the bright and morning star.**" Christ said, "I Jesus… am…the…morning star." Are the new English Bibles trying to make Jesus Christ and Satan the same?

DANIEL 3:25

He answered and said, Lo, I see four men loose,
walking in the midst of the fire, and they have no hurt;
and the form of the fourth is like **the Son of God.**

This is an Old Testament appearance of Jesus Christ. But look at how the modern versions try to present Jesus.

NIV — *a son of the gods*
NASB — *a son of the gods*
NRSV — *a god*
REB — *a god*
LB — *a god*
NWT — *a son of the gods*
NAB — *a son of God* [not the son of God]

Jesus Christ is God. Therefore, He is not a god. The little "g" signifies that He is not the supreme God but is just one of the *pagan* gods.

Jesus Christ is the Son of God. This shows the Deity of Christ and His part in the Trinity. The Trinity has three parts, yet They are all One. These parts are God the Father, God the Son, and God the Holy Spirit. Jesus Christ is God the Son.

Jesus was not just *a* son of God, but He was **the** Son of God. When you use *a* Son of God (or son of God like NAB and versions), it hints that there might be more than one Son. For example, the Mormons believe that Jesus Christ was *a* son of

God… just as much as they believe that Lucifer (Satan) was a son of God! Mormons also believe that each and every one of us is a son of God. That means that Jesus Christ is supposedly our brother. Jesus Christ is not our "brother"; He is our Saviour, God, Lord, and King. One of the most well known verses in the Bible, John 3:16 says, "For God so loved the world that he gave His **only**, begotten Son…" That word "only" means one! This simply tells us that Jesus was the only *one* Son of God.

Jesus was the Son of God… not the Son of gods (or a son of the gods). There is but one God. Jehovah says throughout the book of Isaiah: *"I am the first, and I am the last; and beside me there is no God. Is there a God beside me? yea, there is no God; I know not any…I am the LORD, and there is none else, there is no God beside me: I girded thee, though thou hast not known me."* (Isaiah 44:6b, 8b; 45:5) Mark 12:32 says, *"Thou hast said the truth: for there is one God; and there is none other but he."* Even *the demonic forces* know and believe that there is one God. James 2:19 says, *"Thou believest that there is one God; thou doest well: the devils also believe, and tremble."* You can read in each of the Gospels and see how scared demons were when they came in contact with Jesus Christ. Over and over again, they would proclaim, *"What have we to do with thee, Jesus, thou **Son of God**?"*

Because of their subtle wording, these English [per]versions can be readily accepted by the cults and other religions.

LUKE 2:33

*And **Joseph** and his mother marvelled at those things which were spoken of him.*

By rewording this verse, the new age versions are attacking the virgin birth once again by telling us that Joseph was Christ's father.

NIV — *The child's father*

NASB — *His father*

NRSV — *the child's father*

REB — *The child's father*

NWT — *its* [was Christ not a man?] *father*

NAB — *the child's father*

Christ's "father" was God the Father. Yes, Joseph was His "earthly" father who "raised" Him, but he was **not** His biological father. Miraculously, the Holy Spirit of God planted the seed of the Messiah in Mary's womb.

ACTS 8:37

And Philip said, If thou believest with all thine heart, thou mayest. And he answered and said, I believe that Jesus Christ is the Son of God.

This verse in the Bible teaches that one must be saved before he can be baptized. Many new age versions totally remove this entire verse from the Bible.

NIV — *entire verse missing*

NRSV — *entire verse missing*

REB — *entire verse missing*

NWT — *entire verse missing*

NAB — *omits entire verse* (but renumbers the verses so you won't miss it)

Now, according to new English Bibles, all that one has to do in order to be saved is to get baptized! Salvation by baptism is widely accepted by religions and denominations and is used in many cults today. These kinds of religions and cults would use the modern English Bibles because they blend right in with what they believe and not with what the true Bible teaches.

II CORINTHIANS 2:17

*For we are not as many, which **corrupt** the word of God: but as of sincerity, but as of God, in the sight of God speak we in Christ.*

I wonder if this verse was a "thorn in their flesh" as they were busy "corrupting" the Word of God day and night in their translations. I wonder if they changed the wording of this verse so they could ease their conscience.

NIV — *peddle*

NASB — *peddling*

NRSV — *peddlers*

NWT — *peddlers*

NAB — *trade on the word of God*

NKJV — *peddling*

REB — *adulterating the word of God for profit*
(at least these translators were honest…)

The word "peddle" means "to tinker," or "to play around with." Now it sound like a less serious offence than what it really is. In all actuality, God counts it *very* serious. Not only does God *call* it "corruption," but also He casts **damnation** upon those who perversely change His Word. In Revelation 22:18-19, God solemnly swears, "For I testify unto every man that heareth the words of the prophecy of this book, If any man shall add unto these things, God shall add unto him the plagues that are written in this book: And if any man shall take away from the words of the book of this prophecy, God shall take away his part out of the book of life, and out of the holy city, and from the things which are written in this book." God takes it very seriously. Don't play around with changing His Word *or even join those that want to*. How do we not join them? By not buying their [per]versions of the Bible and by sharing with others the major doctrinal errors in these corrupt Bibles.

COLOSSIANS 1:14

*In whom we have **redemption through his blood,
even the forgiveness of sins:***

Satan hates the atoning blood of the Lord Jesus Christ with fervent passion because it is the blood of Christ that perverts him from dragging saved sinners into Hell with him. Therefore, we should not be surprised to find that the blood of Christ is missing in modern translations.

NIV — *redemption, the forgiveness of sins*

NASB — *redemption, the forgiveness of sins*

NRSV — *redemption, the forgiveness of sins*

REB — *our release is secured and our sins are forgiven*

NWT — *we have our release by ransom, the forgiveness of sins*

NAB — *redemption, the forgiveness of our sins*

The blood atonement of Jesus Christ is another fundamental of the faith, and Satan is working his dead level best to knock this tremendous truth and saving fact down *because* as the King James Bible—the only inspired Word of God for the English speaking people—reads: "We have redemption through his blood." Hebrews 9:12 even says that "[n]either by the blood of goats and calves, but by his own blood he [Jesus] entered in once into the holy place, having obtained eternal redemption for us." I John 1:7 reads, "The blood of Jesus Christ his Son cleanseth us from all sin." Friend, it is through the shed blood of Christ that we might be saved.

Why do you think that there was so much shedding of blood in the animal sacrifices back in Old Testament times? Because it was a representation of what Christ would do some day for us by shedding His good red blood on an old rugged Cross! With His blood, Jesus purchased God's gift of eternal life for you and for me, He made the salvation plan complete, and He paid for all the sins of the world. It was all made clear on Calvary.

I TIMOTHY 6:20

*O Timothy, keep that which is committed to thy trust, avoiding profane and vain babblings, and oppositions of **science** falsely so called:*

Many lies are being propagated today in the name of "science," such as evolution, among others. Instead of calling it a "science," new versions call it a "knowledge."

NIV — *knowledge*

NASB — *knowledge*

NRSV — *knowledge*

REB — *knowledge*

LB — *knowledge*

NWT — *knowledge*

NAB — *knowledge*

NKJV — *knowledge*

With the new version translations, it makes evolution more acceptable as a "science" in the eyes of others, since it supposedly is more than just "knowledge." However, the Word of God (our King James Bible) warns us and commands us in I Timothy 6:20 to avoid them.

II TIMOTHY 2:15

Study to shew thyself approved unto God, a workman that needeth not to be ashamed, rightly dividing the word of truth.

This verse commands us to "study" and to "rightly divide" the Word of God. Of course, the Devil doesn't like that or appreciate it one bit. So what does he do? He changes it.

NIV — *Do your best...correctly handles*

NASB — *Be diligent...handling accurately*

NRSV — *Do your best...rightly explaining*

REB — *Try hard...keep strictly to the true gospel*

LB — *Work hard...Know what his word says and means*

NWT — *Do your utmost...handling the word of truth aright*

NAB — *Try hard...following a straight course in preaching the truth*

NKJV — *Be diligent...rightly dividing*

I JOHN 5:7

For there are three that bear record in heaven, the Father, the Word, and the Holy Ghost: and these three are one.

This is one of the most powerful verses in the Bible that clearly defines the Trinity. Follow my deductive reasoning of the Trinity.

SCRIPTURAL PROOF OF THE TRINITY

The Statements	The Reasons
1. the Father = *God*	Isaiah 63:16, 64:8
2. the Holy Spirit = *God*	Acts 5:3-4
3. Jesus Christ = *God*	Psalm 102:24-27 Hebrews 1:8,10-12
4. the Father + the Holy Spirit + Jesus Christ = *God*	(connected through given reasons)
5. the Father + the Holy Spirit + Jesus Christ = *the Trinity* [three, yet equal, still One]	I John 5:7

The shocking truth is that I John 5:7 has been **completely** **removed** *from all the new English versions of the Bible!*

CONCLUSION

Our study of how modern English translations are reworded, eliminating key doctrine and adding error, has been very brief. There is *much more* that we could have discussed.

Satan is the Father of perversion. *Satan loves changing the Word of God.* Do you think God is would try to mess with our minds and continually change His Word on us? *No.* There is a **big** difference between the King James Bible and all the other English versions. The King James Bible comes from the accurate, accepted Hebrew and Greek texts; while, in all reality, the new English versions come from corrupt texts compiled by followers of Satan.

God counts His Word to be very precious, holy, and perfect; and He does not want anybody to mess around with it. In the beginning, the middle, and the end of His inspired Book, He has given a warning to those who mess with His Word. God speaks in Deuteronomy 12:32, "What thing soever I command you, observe to do it: *thou **shalt not** add thereto, nor diminish from it.*" He again warns in Proverbs 30:5-6, "Every word of God is pure…. *Add thou **not** unto his words.*" God's word is pure, and He does not need man's filthy fingers playing with it! As Dr. Jack Hyles use to say, "Keep your stinkin' feet out of my drinking water!" Only three verses from the end of the entire Bible, God warns us again in Revelation 22:18, "If any man shall add unto these things, God *shall* add unto him the plagues that are written in this book." Five of the new English Bible version editors have lost their ability to speak. *God has kept His word.*

We must be careful. There are differences between the King James Version and the modern English translations. Not only in where they came from textually, but also doctrinally. It is evident that these modern translations are corrupted Bibles – but the King James Version is the preserved, inspired Word of God.

WHAT OTHERS HAVE SAID ABOUT THE BIBLE

This chapter is a compilation of what other men and women of humanity's past have said about God's inspired, preciously preserved, holy Word. These are some tremendous quotes.

"So great is my veneration for the Bible that the earlier my children begin to read it the more confident will be my hope that they will prove useful citizens of their country and respectable members of society. I have for many years made it a practice to read through the Bible once every year." – *John Quincy Adams*

"Gentlemen, in this Book [the Bible] will be found the solution of all the problems of the world." – *Calvin Coolidge*

"All I know of good, truth, honesty, and idealism I have learned from the Bible. In school I listened each morning as a chapter was read before classes started, and it was then that I came to know and respect the Holy Book. I never have lost my regard for the Word of God, and if

I had my way about it, a chapter of the Bible would be read every single morning in every school in this country. I feel at home in the pages of the Bible, for that Book speaks my language." – *Henry Ford*

"The Bible is the sheet-anchor of our liberties." – *Ulysses S. Grant*

"It is impossible to enslave mentally or socially a Bible-reading people. The principles of the Bible are the groundwork of human freedom." – *Horace Greeley*

"Here is a Book, the Bible, worth more than all others that were ever printed; yet it is my misfortune never to have found time to read it." – *Patrick Henry, near death*

"The whole of the inspirations of our civilization springs from the teachings of Christ and the lessons of the prophets. To read the Bible for these fundamentals is a necessity of American life." – *Herbert Hoover*

"The Bible is the unfailing guide which points the way for men to the perfect life. The lessons of charity, justice, and equality which enrich its pages should be learned well by all men in order that greed, avarice, and iniquity can be blotted out." – *J. Edgar Hoover*

"That book [the Bible], sir, is the rock on which our republic rests." – *Andrew Jackson*

"Forty years I have loved the Word of God. I feel the blessed pages under my hand with special thankfulness, as a rod and a staff to keep my steps firm through the valley of shadow of depression and world calamity. Truly, the Bible, the teaching of our Savior, is the 'only way out of the dark.'" – *Helen Keller*

"Unless we form the habit of going to the Bible in bright moments as well as in trouble, we cannot fully respond to its consolations, because we lack equilibrium between light and darkness." – *Helen Keller*

"The Bible, a book in comparison with which, in my eyes, all others are of minor importance, has never failed to give me strength." – *Robert E. Lee*

"In all my perplexities and distresses, the Bible has never failed to give me light and strength." – *Robert E. Lee*

"I believe the Bible is the best gift God has ever given to man. All the good from the Savior of the world is communicated to us through that book." – *Abraham Lincoln*

"Believe me, sir, never a night goes by, be I ever so tired, but I read the Word of God before I go to bed." – *Douglas MacArthur*

"I have made large purchases of property in my time involving millions of dollars; but it was as a boy that I made my greatest purchase. That little red Book [Bible] was the foundation on which my life has been built and has made possible all that has counted in my life. I know now that it was the greatest investment and the most important purchase I ever made." – *John Wanamaker*

"It is impossible to rightly govern the world without God and the Bible." – *George Washington*

"If there is anything in my thoughts or style to commend, the credit is due to my parents for instilling in me an early love of the Scriptures. If we abide by the principles taught in the Bible, our country will go on prospering and to prosper; but if we and our posterity neglect its instructions and authority, no man can tell how sudden a catastrophe may overwhelm us and bury all our glory in profound obscurity." – *Daniel Webster*

"If there is aught of eloquence in me, it is because I learned the Scriptures at my mother's knee." – *Daniel Webster*

"The Bible is the chief moral cause of all that is *good,* and the best corrector of all that is *evil,* in human society; the *best* book for regulating the temporal concerns of men, and the *only book* that can serve as an infallible guide to future felicity." – *Noah Webster*

"The Bible is the Word of life—it is a picture of the human heart displayed for all ages and all sorts of conditions of men. I feel sorry for the men who do not read the Bible every day. I wonder why they deprive themselves of the strength and pleasure." – *Woodrow Wilson*

"When you have read the Bible, you will know it is the Word of God, because you will have found it the key to your own heart, your own happiness and your own duty." – *Woodrow Wilson*

"There is no philosophy like that of the Scriptures." – *Lord Bacon*

"No better lessons can I teach my child than those of the Bible." – *Denis Diderot*

"Young man, my advice to you is that you cultivate an acquaintance with and firm belief in the Holy Scriptures, for this is your certain interest. I think Christ's system of morals and religion, as He left them to us, is the best the world ever saw or is likely to see." – *Benjamin Franklin*

"It is a belief in the Bible which has served me as the guide of my moral and literary life… The farther the ages advance in civilization the more will the Bible be used." – *Johann Wolfgang von Goethe*

"Peruse the books of philosophers with all their pomp of diction. How meager, how contemptible are they when compared with the Scriptures! The majesty of the Scriptures strikes me with admiration." – *Jean Jacques Rousseau*

"The Bible is the charter of all true liberty, the forerunner of all civilizations, the molder of institutions and governments, the fashion of law, the secret of national progress, the guide of history, the ornament and mainspring of literature, the inspiration of philosophies, the text-book of ethics, the light of the intellect, the soul of all strong heart life, the illuminator of darkness, the foe of superstition, the enemy of oppression, the uprooter of sin, the comfort in sorrow, the strength in weakness, the pathway in perplexity, the escape from temptation, the steadier in the day of power, the embodiment of all lofty ideals, the begetter of life, the promise of the future, the star of death's night, the revealer of God, the guide and the hope and the inspiration of man." – *William F. Anderson*

"I know the Bible is inspired because it inspires me." – *Dwight Lyman Moody*

"What makes the difference is not how many times you have been through the Bible, but how many times and how thoroughly the Bible has been through you." – *Gypsy Smith*

"Be walking Bibles." – *Charles Spurgeon*

"The Bible is a harbor where I can drop down my anchor, feeling certain that it will hold. Here is a place where I can find sure footing; and, by the grace of God, from this confidence I shall never be moved." – *Charles Spurgeon*

"Perhaps there is no book more neglected in these days than the Bible. I believe there are moldier Bibles in this world than there are of any sort of neglected books. We have no book that is so much bought, and then so speedily laid aside and so little used, as the Bible." – *Charles Spurgeon*

"What scenery it is through which the Christian man walks—the towering mountains of prophecy, the great sea of providence, the might cliffs of divine promise, the green fields of divine grace, the river that makes glad the city of God—oh, what scenery surrounds the Christian, and what fresh discoveries he makes at ever step! The Bible is always a new book. If you want a novel, read your Bible; it is always new; there is not a stale page in the Word of God; it is just as fresh as though the ink were not yet dry, but had flowed today from the pen of inspiration. There have been poets whose saying startled all England when first their verses were thrown broadcast over the land, but nobody reads their writings now; yet the pages that were written by David and by Paul are glowing with the radiant glory which was upon them when long ago the Holy Spirit spake by them." – *Charles Spurgeon*

"I will give ten reasons why I believe the Bible is the Word of God. (1) On the ground of the Testimony of Jesus Christ. (2) On the ground of its fulfilled prophecies. (3) On the ground of the unity of the Book. When 66 books, written by some 40 authors, through 1,500 years or more, and in different countries, provide a book without a single contradiction and united on the great doctrines and principles taught, that has to be supernatural. (4) On the ground of the immeasurable superiority of the teachings of the Bible to those of any other and all other books. (5) On the ground of the history of the Book, its victory over attack. (6) On the ground of the character of those who accept and those who reject the Book. (7) On the ground of the influence of the Book. (8) On the ground of the inexhaustible depth of the Book. (9) On the ground of the fact that as we grow in knowledge and holiness, we grow toward the Bible. (10) On the ground of the direct testimony of the Holy Spirit." – *R. A. Torrey*

"Why will people go astray when they have this blessed Book to guide them?" – *Michael Faraday*

"All human discoveries seem to be made only for the purpose of confirming more strongly the truths contained in the Holy Scriptures." – *Sir William Herschel*

"The chief aim of all investigations of the external world should be to discover the rational order and harmony which has been imposed on it by God and which He revealed to us in the language of mathematics." – *Johannes Kepler*

"If all the great books of the world were given life and were brought together in Convention, the moment the Bible entered, the other books would fall on their faces as the gods of Philistia fell when the ark of God was brought into their presence in the temple of Dagon." – *Sir Isaac Newton*

"This Book contains the mind of God, the state of man, the way of salvation, the doom of sinners, and the happiness of believers. Its doctrines are holy, its precepts are binding, its histories are true, and its decisions are immutable. Read it to be wise, believe it to be saved, and practice it to be holy. It contains light to direct you, food to support you, and comfort to cheer you. It is the traveler's map, the pilot's compass, the soldier's sword, and the Christian's charter. It is a mine of wealth, a paradise of glory, and a river of pleasure." – *Author Unknown*

"The Bible is a beautiful palace built up out of sixty-six blocks of solid marble. In the first chapter of Genesis we enter the Vestibule, which is filled with the mighty acts of Creation. The Vestibule gives access to the law courts, the five books of Moses, passing through which we come to the picture gallery of the historical books. Here we find hung upon the walls scenes of battlefields, representations of heroic deeds, and portraits of eminent men belonging to the early days of the world's history. Beyond the picture gallery we find the philosopher's chamber, the book of Job, passing through which we enter the music room, the book of Psalms where we listen to the grandest strains that ever fell on human ears. Then we come to the business office, the book of Proverbs where, right in the center of the room, stand facing us the motto, "Righteousness Exalteth a Nation, but Sin Is a Reproach to Any People." From the business office we pass into the chapel. Ecclesiastes, or the preacher in his pulpit and thence into the conservatory—the Song of Solomon with Rose of Sharon and the Lily of the Valley, and all manner of fine perfume and fruits and flowers and singing birds. Finally we reach the observatory, the Prophets, with their telescopes fixed on near distant stars, and all directed toward "The Bright and Morning Star" that soon is to arise. Crossing the courts we come to the audience chamber of the King, the Gospels, where we find our vivid-like portraits of the King Himself. Next we enter the word room of the Holy Spirit, the Acts of the Apostles and beyond that the correspondence room—

the Peter, James, John, and Jude busy at their desks, and if you would know what they are writing about, their epistles are open for all to study. Before leaving we stand for a moment in the outside gallery, The Revelation of Jesus Christ, where we look upon some striking pictures of the judgments to come, and the glories to be revealed, concluding with an awe inspiring picture of the throne room of the King of kings and Lord of lords." – *Author Unknown*

"Yet it [the Bible] lives! Generation follows generation—yet it lives. Nations rise and fall—yet it lives. Kings, dictators, presidents come and go—yet it lives. Hated, despised, cursed—yet it lives. Doubted, suspected, criticized—yet it lives. Condemned by atheists—yet it lives. Scoffed at by scorners—yet it lives. Exaggerated by fanatics—yet it lives. Misconstrued and misstated—yet it lives. Ranted and raved about—yet it lives. Its inspiration denied—yet it lives. Yet it lives—as a lamp to our feet. Yet it lives—as a light to our path. Yet it lives—as the gate to heaven. Yet it lives—as a standard for childhood. Yet it lives—as a guide for youth. Yet it lives—as an inspiration for the matured. Yet it lives—as a comfort for the aged. Yet it lives—as a food for the hungry. Yet it lives—as rest for the weary. Yet it lives—as a light for the heathen. Yet it lives—as salvation for the sinner. Yet it lives—as grace for the Christian. To know it is to love it. To love it is to accept it. To accept it means life eternal." – *Author Unknown*

"This deathless Book has survived three great dangers: the negligence of its friends; the false systems built upon it; and the warfare of those who have hated it." – *Author Unknown*

"A young Christian packing his bag for a journey said to a friend, 'I have nearly finished packing. All I have to put in are a guidebook, a lamp, a mirror, a microscope, a telescope, a volume of fine poetry, a few biographies, a package of old letters, a book of songs, a sword, a hammer, and a set of tools.' 'But you cannot put all that into your bag,' objected the friend. 'Oh, yes,' said the Christian. 'Here it is.' And he placed his Bible in the corner of the suitcase and closed the lid." – *Author Unknown, related by Tennessee Ernie Ford*

"Scholars may quote Plato in their studies, but the hearts of millions will quote the Bible at their daily toil, and draw strength from its inspiration, as the meadows draw it from the brook." – *Conway*

"The Scriptures teach us the best way of living, the noblest way of suffering, and the most comfortable way of dying." – *Flavel*

"The highest earthly enjoyments are but a shadow of the joy I find I reading God's word." – *Grey*

"No one ever graduates from Bible study until he meets the Author face to face." – *Harris*

"If God is a reality and the soul is a reality, and you are an immortal being, what are you doing with your Bible shut!" – *Johnson*

"I found long since that as I allowed the pressure of professional and worldly engagements to fill in every moment between rising and going to bed, the spirit would surely starve. So I made a rule, which I have since stuck to in spite of many temptations, not to read or study anything but my Bible after the evening meal, and never to read any other book but the Bible on the Sabbath. I do not exclude real Bible helps which always drive one back to the Bible, but I never spend time simply on devotional books. Since making this resolution, God in His mercy has shown me that His Word is an inexhaustible storehouse, from which He dispenses rich stores of precious truths to His servants as He pleases, and as they are ready to receive them." – *Howard A. Kelly, physician*

"If all the neglected Bibles were dusted simultaneously, we would have a record dust storm and the sun would go into eclipse for a whole week." – *Nygren*

"I believe a knowledge of the Bible without a college course is more valuable than a college course without a Bible." – *William Lyon Phelps*

"Bring me the book." (He was then asked, "What book?" He replied,) "There is only one book—the Bible." – *Sir Walter Scott*

"The devil can cite Scripture for his purpose." – *William Shakespeare*

"Conscience tells us that we ought to do right, but it does not tell us what right is—that we are taught by God's Word." – *H. C. Trumbull*

"What is the secret of England's superiority among the nations? Go tell your prince that this [the Bible] is the secret of England's political greatness." – *Queen Victoria of England*

CONCLUSION

It is very important to know why the Bible is God's inspired, preserved Word. I pray that you now have a good working knowledge of what we have talked about in our discussion about the Bible:

- *How the Bible has been inspired of God*

- *Why the Bible truly is the inspired Word of God through various proofs and evidences*

- *How God has preserved His Word*

- *How the Apocryphal books could not have been inspired*

- *Why our King James Bible is the inspired, preserved Word of God for the English-speaking people*

- *Why all the modern English versions of the Bible are not the correct translations of the Word of God*

I pray that you will take to heart all that we have discussed and use it for the glory of God. Use it to always keep yourself in check regarding this topic so that you might not sin against God by turning from your complete faith and trust in the King James Bible to accept a different, non-Inspired, non-Preserved English [per]version of the Holy Scriptures. Besides this, use this book to edify the brethren when need be concerning this entire issue, and reveal to them the truth of the trail of the KJV's original roots and how it is the only Inspired, preserved Word of God for the English speaking people.

Truly, our Bible—the *King James* Bible—is our Blessed Book. Love it. Cherish it. Read it. Protect it. Learn from it. Muse upon it. Talk about it. Keep it. Share it with a lost and dying world.

My friend, Paul gives us a charge in I Corinthians 15:58 that I would like to pass on to you. He tells us: "Therefore, my beloved brethren, *be ye* **steadfast, unmoveable...** "Let me challenge you to be *established* in the truth that the Bible *is* God's Word. Be *unmovable* in the truth that the King James Bible is our only inspired, preserved Word.

Years from now, after you have lived your Christian life and you're about to approach the days when you will enter into Heaven through the White Pearly Gates, may you be able to look back over your life and truly and confidently say as Paul did: "I have fought a good fight, I have finished my course, *I have kept the faith...*"

Meet The Author

Caleb Garraway was born into a Christian home on July 20, 1986 and was born into the family of God on November 9, 1994. At the age of 11, he was called to preach through the preaching of Dr. Jack Hyles at Pastor's School in Hammond, IN. While attending Oklahoma Baptist College, Caleb traveled on the men's singing group for four years and also worked at the Windsor Hills Baptist Church for two years.

God has burdened his heart with America—its young people and its lost souls. Through his evangelism ministry, he desires to stir up the hearts of American Christians to zealously reach the next generation before it is too late and to challenge young people to maintain the Cause for our Lord Jesus Christ. Many souls have been saved and many lives have been touched by his ministry.

Caleb and Katie were married on March 20, 2010. Pray for them as they travel—for Holy Spirit power, Holy Spirit passion, and lost souls to be rescued from the flames of Hell and added to the church.

CONTACT CALEB GARRAWAY AT:
prophetproductionsobc@gmail.com or 917.412.0059

www.thegarrawayfamily.com

Breinigsville, PA USA
05 November 2010
248683BV00006B/2/P